Jean-Claude Corbeil
Ariane Archambault

My First FRENCH • ENGLISH VISUAL DICTIONARY

FIREFLY BOOKS

A Firefly Book

Published by Firefly Books Ltd. 2006

First printing

Publisher Cataloging-in-Publication Data (U.S.)

Corbeil, Jean-Claude.

My first French English visual dictionary/Jean-Claude Corbeil ; Ariane Archambeault.

(80) p. : col. ill. ; cm.

Includes index.

Summary: A general reference visual dictionary for young children featuring terms in English and French.

ISBN-13: 978-1-55407-193-7
ISBN-10: 1-55407-193-3

1. Picture dictionaries, French—Juvenile literature. 2. Picture dictionaries, English—Juvenile literature. 3. French language—Dictionaries—English—Juvenile literature. 4. English language—Dictionaries—French—Juvenile literature. I. Archambeault, Ariane. II. Title.

443.21 dc22 PC2629.C6736 2006

Library and Archives Canada Cataloguing in Publication

Corbeil, Jean-Claude, 1932-

My first French English visual dictionary/Jean-Claude Corbeil, Ariane Archambault.

Includes index.

ISBN-13: 978-1-55407-193-7
ISBN-10: 1-55407-193-3

1. Picture dictionaries, French—Juvenile literature. 2. Picture dictionaries, English—Juvenile literature. 3. French language—Dictionaries, Juvenile—English. 4. English language—Dictionaries, Juvenile—French. I. Archambault, Ariane, 1936- II. Title.

AG250.C66386 2006 j443'.21 C2006-900747-0

Published in the United States by
Firefly Books (U.S.) Inc.
P.O. Box 1338, Ellicott Station
Buffalo, New York 14205

Published in Canada by
Firefly Books Ltd.
66 Leek Crescent
Richmond Hill, Ontario
L4B 1H1

Printed in Singapore

My First Visual Dictionary was created and produced by :
QA International
329 de la Commune St. West
3rd floor
H2Y 2E1 Canada
T 514.499.3000 F 514.499.3010
www.qa-international.com

AUTHORS
Jean-Claude Corbeil
Ariane Archambault

PUBLISHER
Caroline Fortin

EDITORIAL DIRECTORS
François Fortin
Martine Podesto

EDITOR-IN-CHIEF
Anne Rouleau

TERMINOLOGICAL RESEARCH
Jean Beaumont
Catherine Briand
Nathalie Guillo

GRAPHIC DESIGN
Éric Millette

COVER AND PAGE SETUP
Josée Noiseux

ILLUSTRATION
Art Director : Jocelyn Gardner
Carl Pelletier
Alain Lemire
Jean-Yves Ahern
Pascal Bilodeau
Yan Bohler
Mélanie Boivin
François Escalmel
Rielle Lévesque
Anouk Noël
Michel Rouleau
Claude Thivierge
Mamadou Togola

DOCUMENTATION
Stéphanie Lanctôt
Gilles Vézina

DATA MANAGEMENT
Programmer: Éric Gagnon
Josée Gagnon

REVISION
Liliane Michaud

PRODUCTION
Nathalie Fréchette

PREPRESS
Guylaine Houle
Pascal Goyette
Sophie Pellerin
Kien Tang

PEDAGOGICAL ADVISER
Roch Turbide

Contents

4 The body
6 The body in motion
8 Clothing
10 At home
12 The bedroom
14 The bathroom
16 The living room
18 The playroom
20 The kitchen
22 The meal
24 Vegetables
26 Fruits
28 The supermarket
30 Familiar animals
32 The farm
34 The forest
36 The desert and the savanna
38 The sea
40 Dinosaurs
42 Plants
44 Space
46 Earth's landscapes
48 The weather
50 Transportation on water
52 Transportation in the air
54 Transportation on land
56 The city
58 Trades
60 School
62 Colors and shapes
64 Numbers and letters
66 Music
68 Sports
70 Camping
72 Parties and holidays
74 Costumes and characters
76 Index

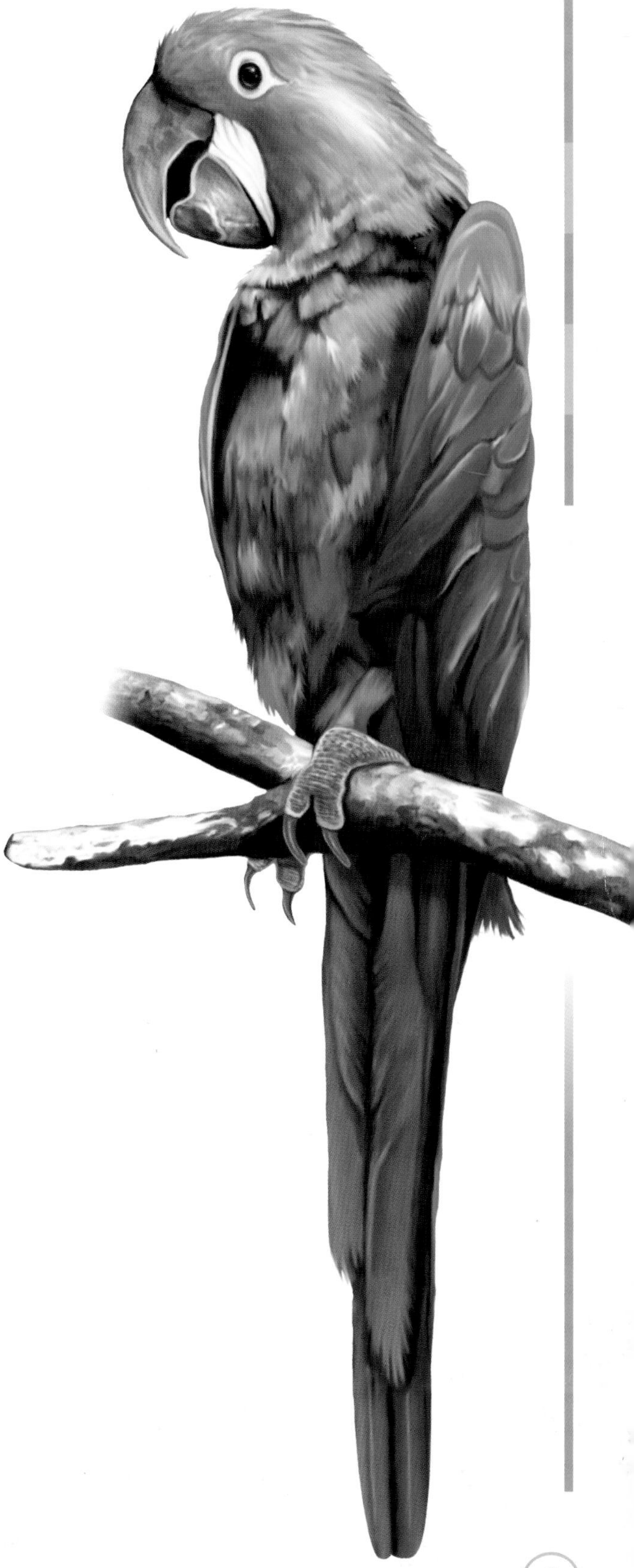

The body
Le corps

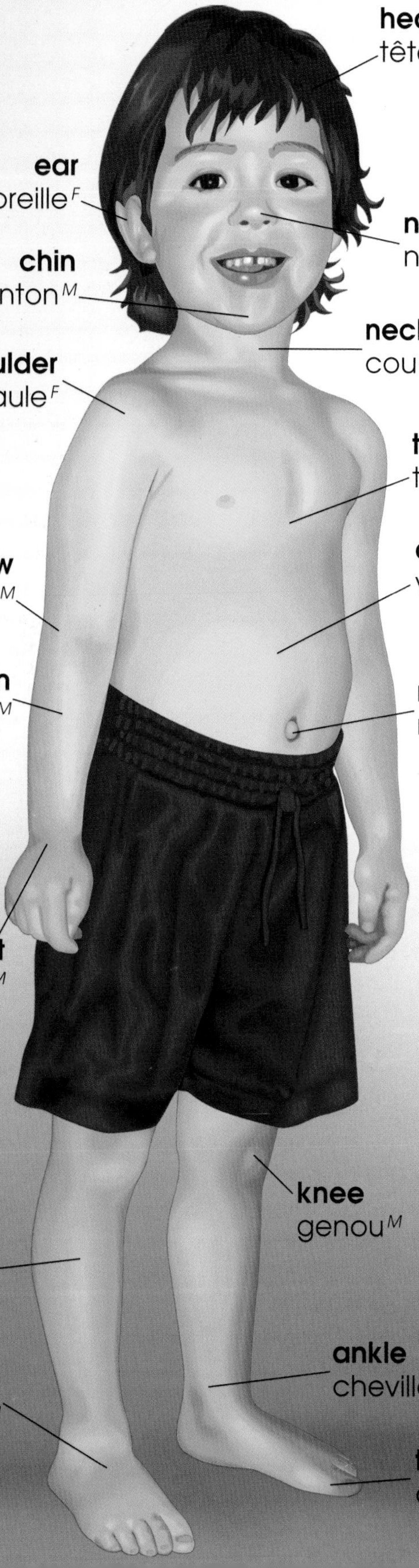

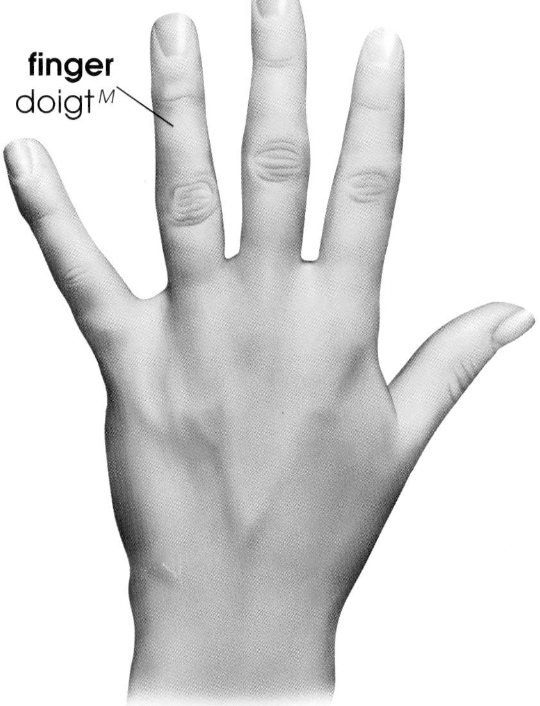

back of the hand
dos[M] de la main[F]

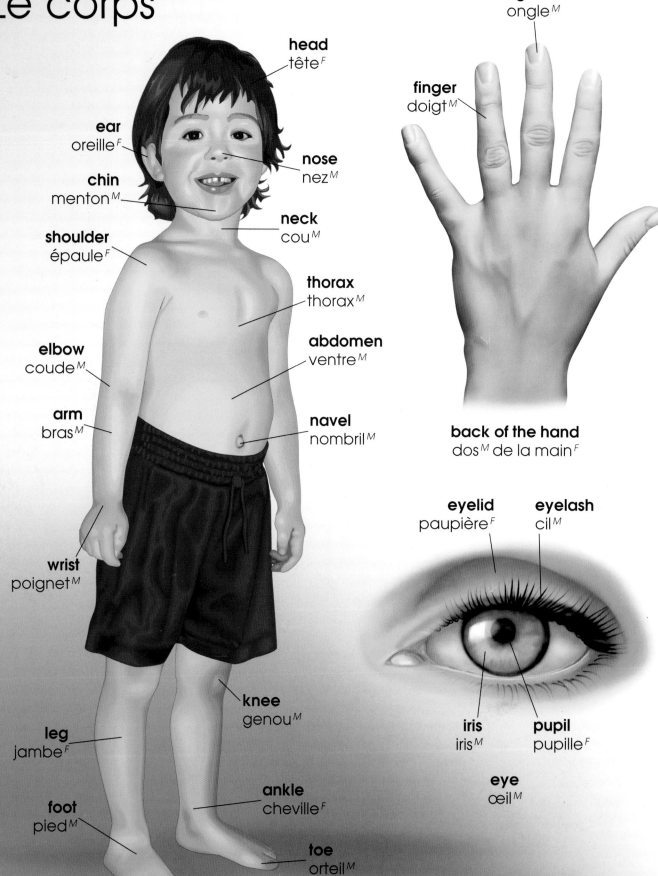

eye
œil[M]

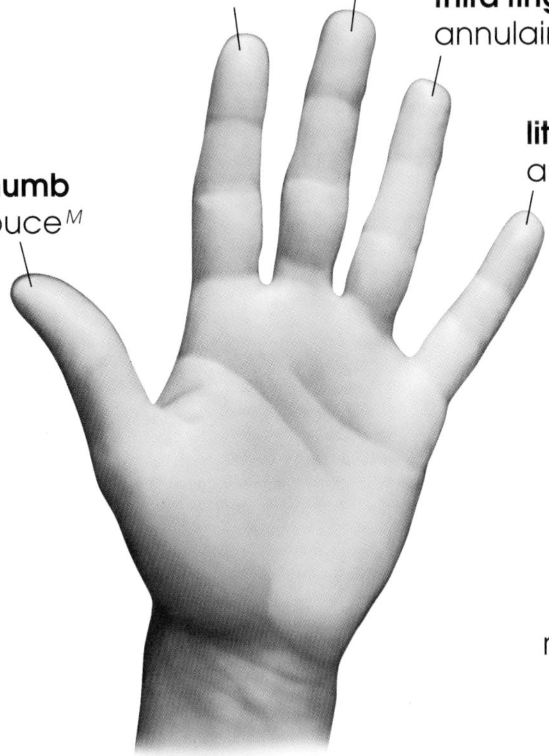

palm of the hand
paume^{F} de la main^{F}

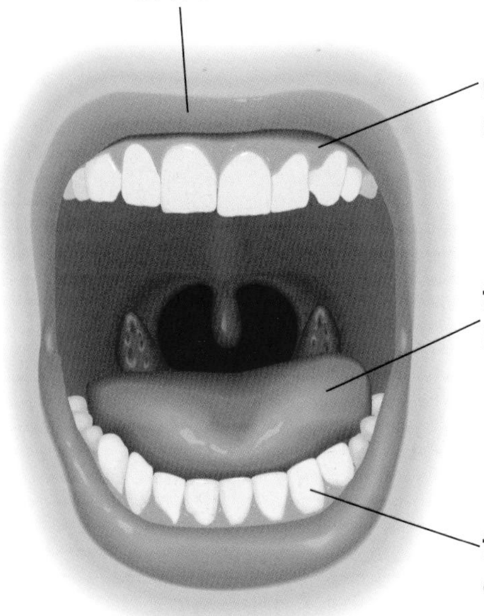

mouth
bouche^{F}

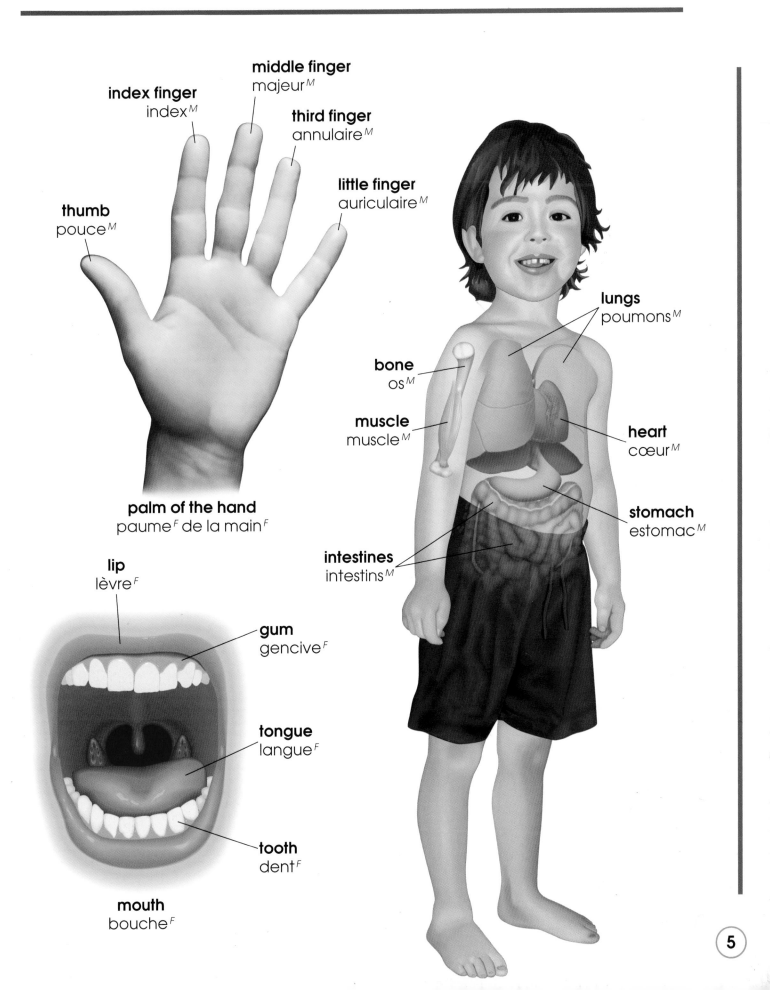

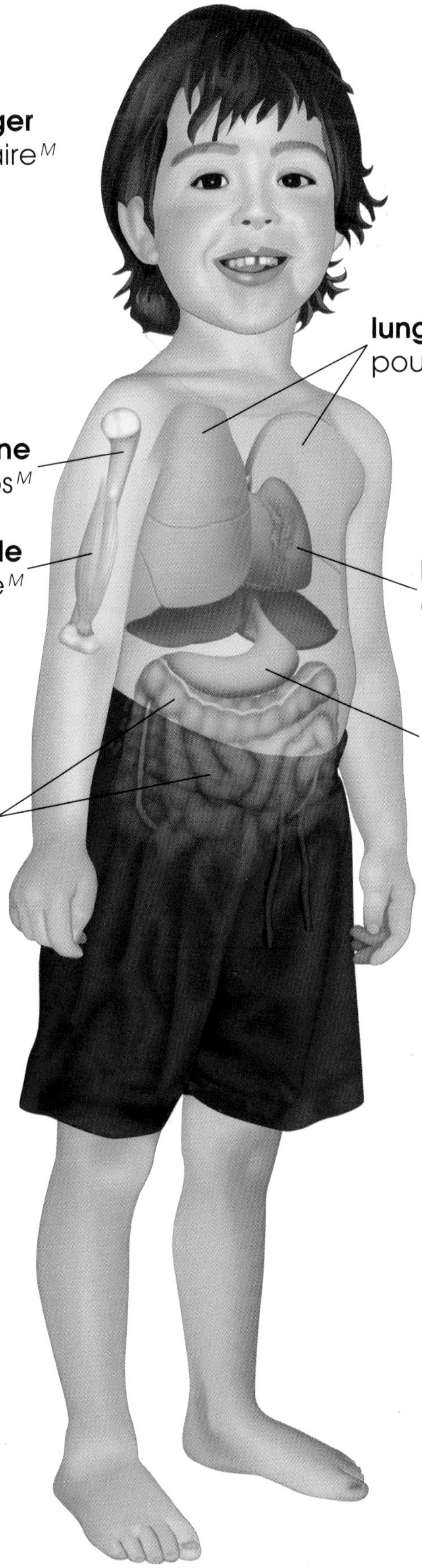

The body in motion
Le corps en mouvement

sit
être assis

walk
marcher

run
courir

jump
sauter

crawl
ramper

sleep
dormir

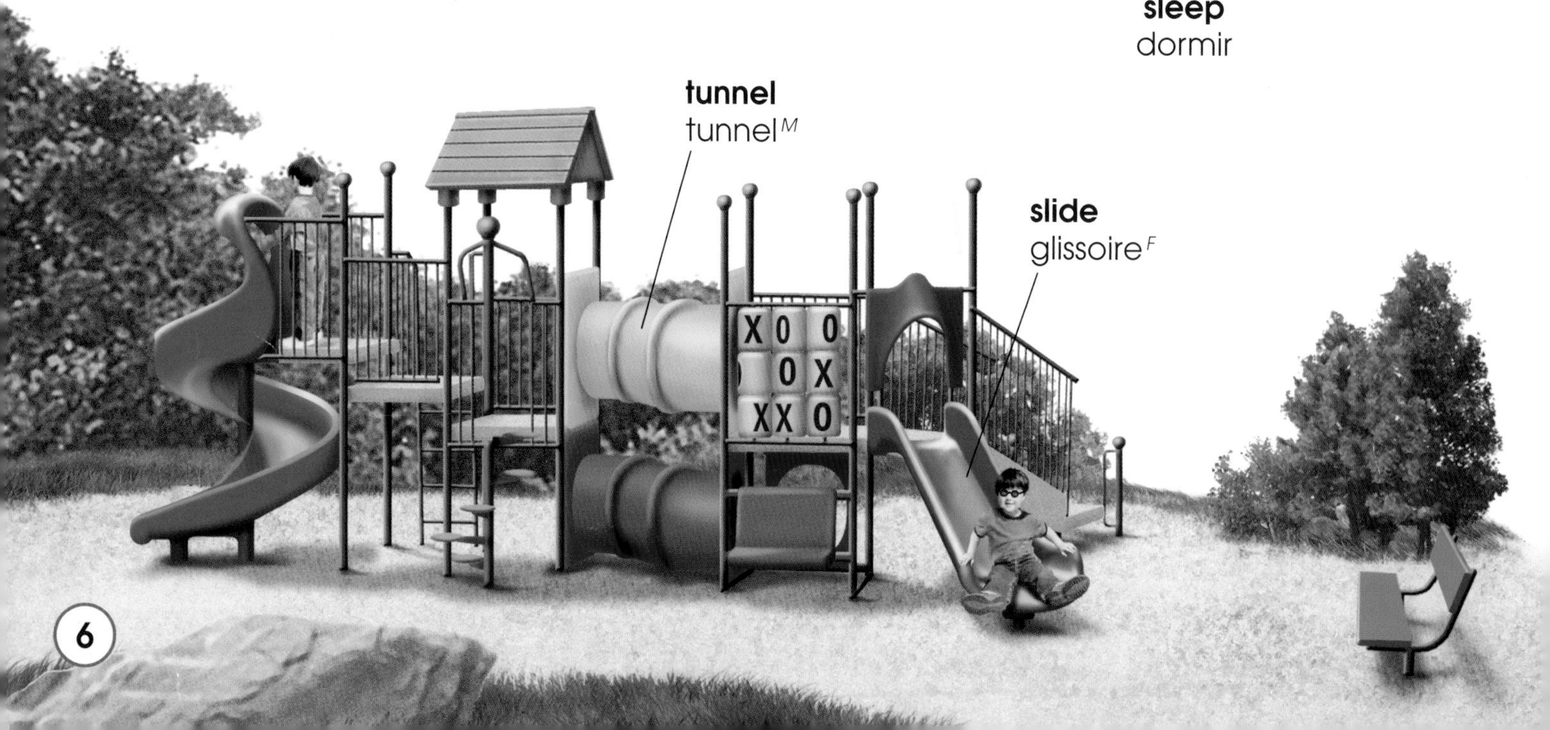

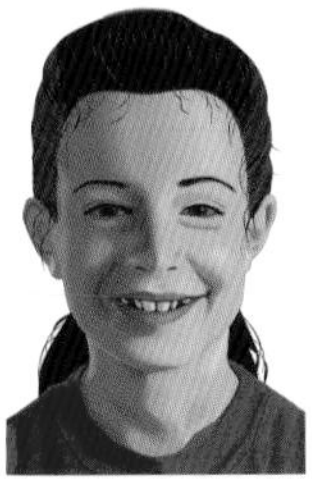

smile
sourire

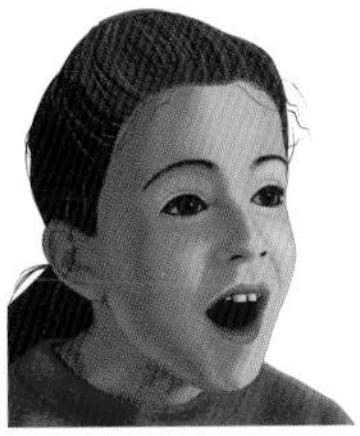

surprised
être surpris

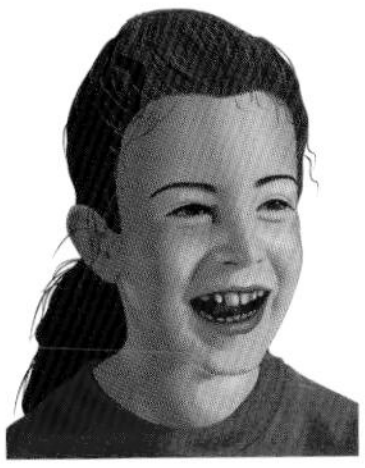

laugh
rire

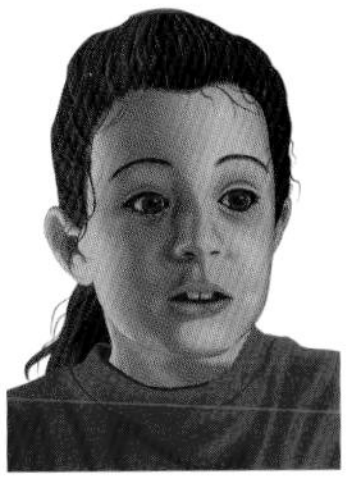

afraid
avoir peur

up
en haut

angry
être fâché

scream
crier

cry
pleurer

in
dans

beside
à côté

down
en bas

in front of
devant

behind
derrière

under
sous

on
sur

Clothing
Les vêtements

running shoe
chaussure[F] de sport[M]

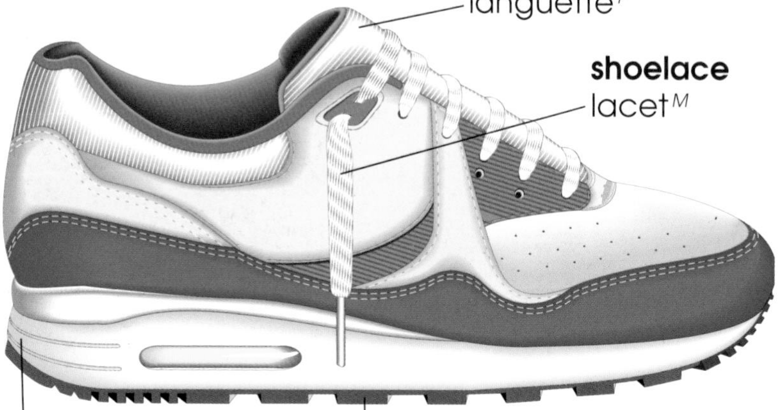

tongue
languette[F]

shoelace
lacet[M]

heel
talon[M]

sole
semelle[F]

knit shirt
polo[M]

sandal
sandale[F]

T-shirt
T-shirt[M]

cardigan
cardigan[M]

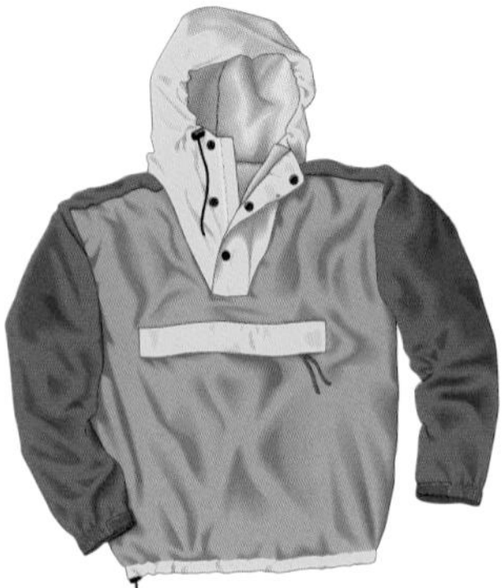

anorak
anorak[M]

turtleneck
col[M] roulé

jeans
jean[M]

strap
bretelle[F]

fly
braguette[F]

overalls
salopette[F]

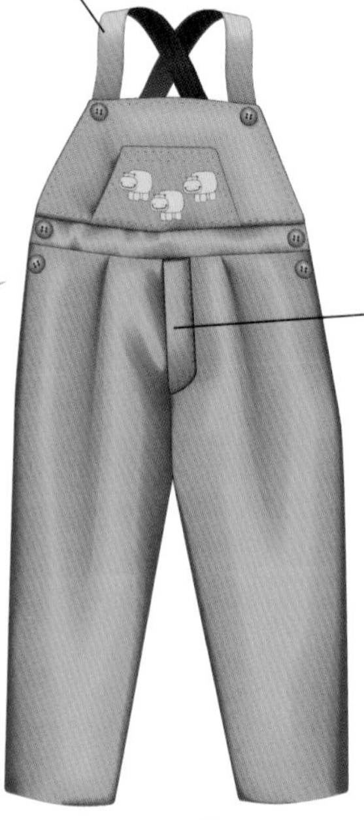

skirt
jupe[F]

dress
robe[F]

necktie
cravate[F]

belt
ceinture[F]

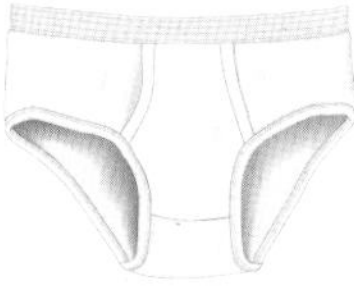

briefs
slip[M]

gloves
gants[M]

shirt
chemise[F]

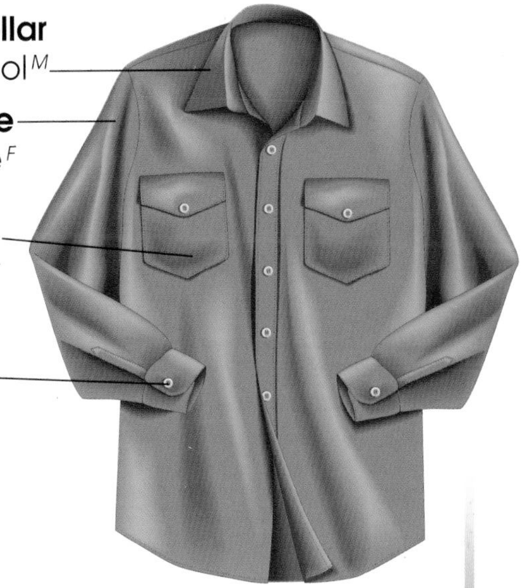

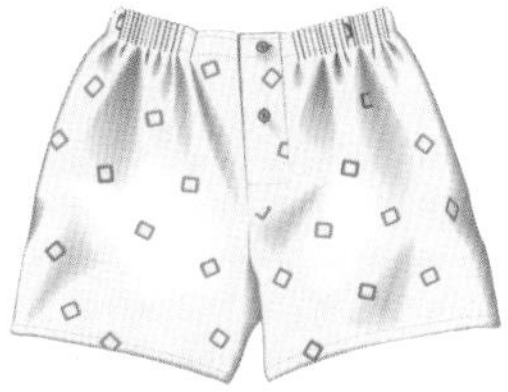

boxer shorts
caleçon[M]

swimsuit
maillot[M] de bain[M]

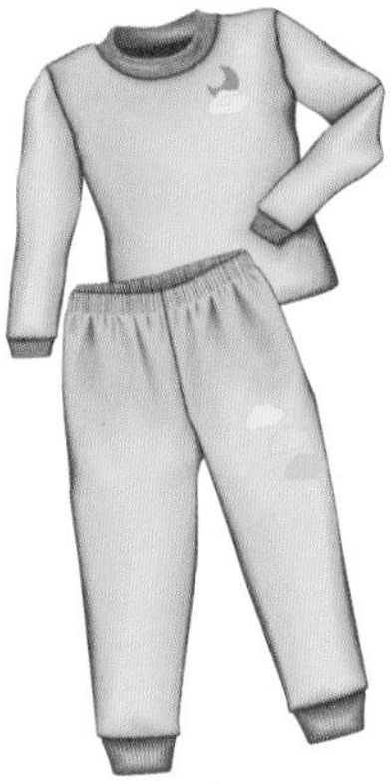

pajamas
pyjama[M]

socks
chaussettes[F]

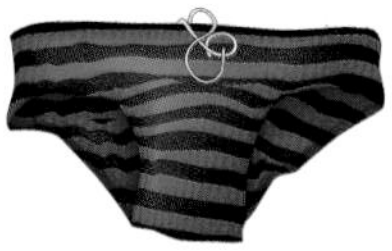

swimming trunks
slip[M] de bain[M]

shorts
short[M]

sweatshirt
pull[M] molletonné

sweatpants
pantalon[M] molletonné

At home
À la maison

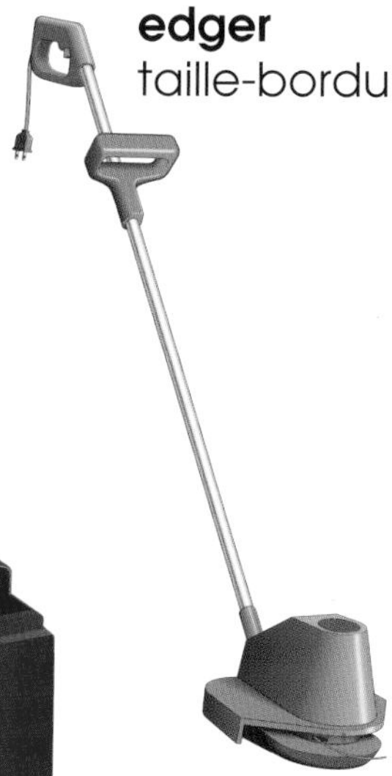

edger
taille-bordures^{M}

tool box
boîte^{F} à outils^{M}

hammer
marteau^{M}

screwdriver
tournevis^{M}

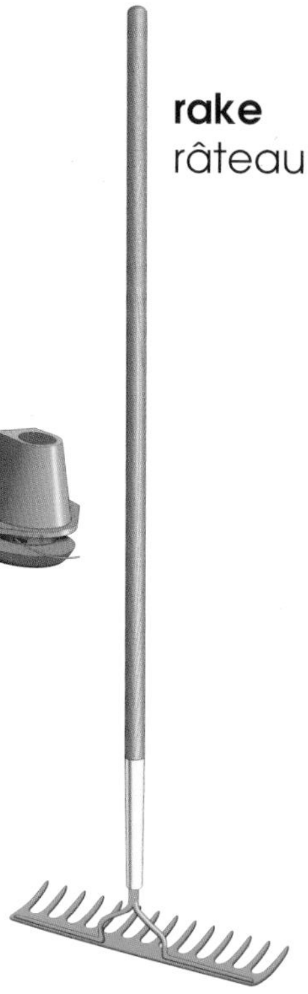

rake
râteau^{M}

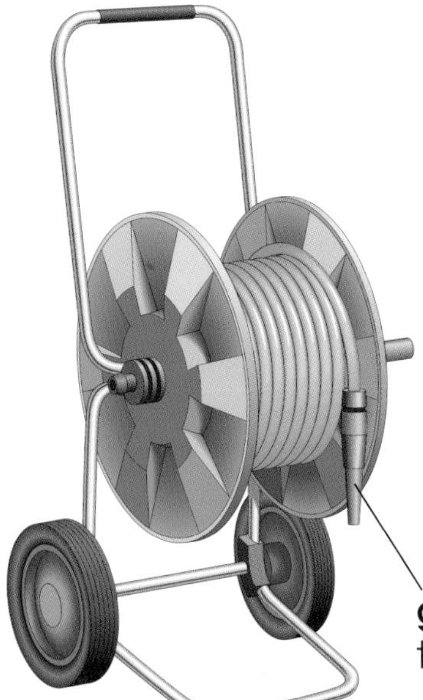

garden hose
tuyau^{M} d'arrosage^{M}

hose trolley
dévidoir^{M} sur roues^{F}

wheelbarrow
brouette^{F}

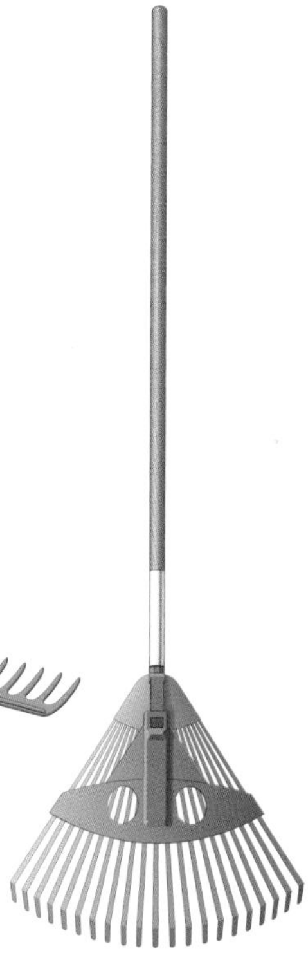

lawn rake
balai^{M} à feuilles^{F}

sprinkler
arroseur^{M}

garbage can
poubelle^{F}

stepladder
escabeau^{M}

mower
tondeuse^{F}

shed
remise^{F}

vegetable garden
jardin^{M} potager

fence
clôture^{F}

lawn
pelouse^{F}

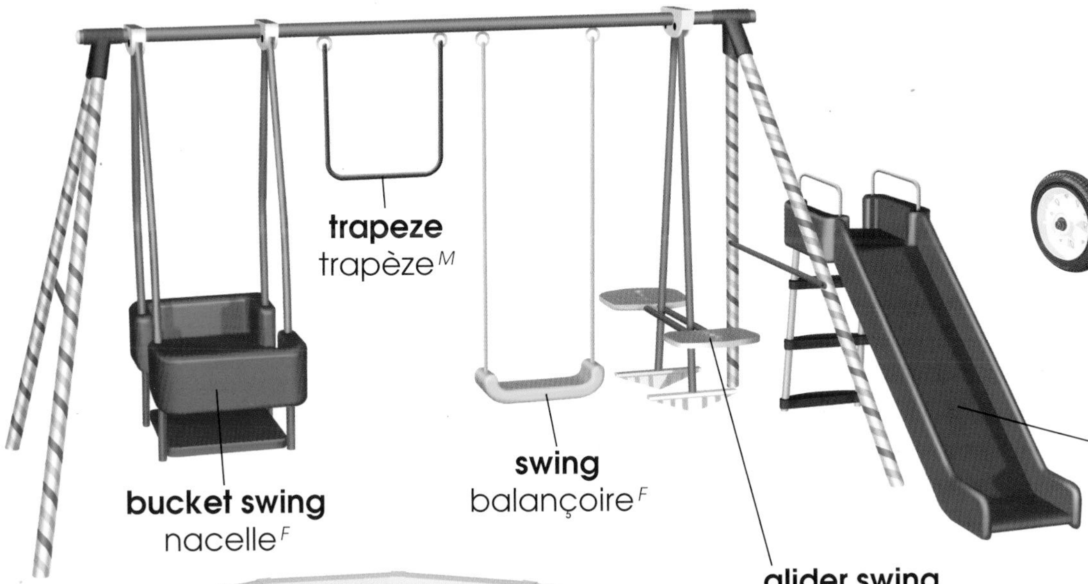
playset
centre[M] d'activités[F]
trapeze
trapèze[M]
bucket swing
nacelle[F]
swing
balançoire[F]
glider swing
balancelle[F] double
slide
glissoire[F]

tricycle
tricycle[M]

above-ground swimming pool
piscine[F] hors sol[M]

wagon
voiturette[F]

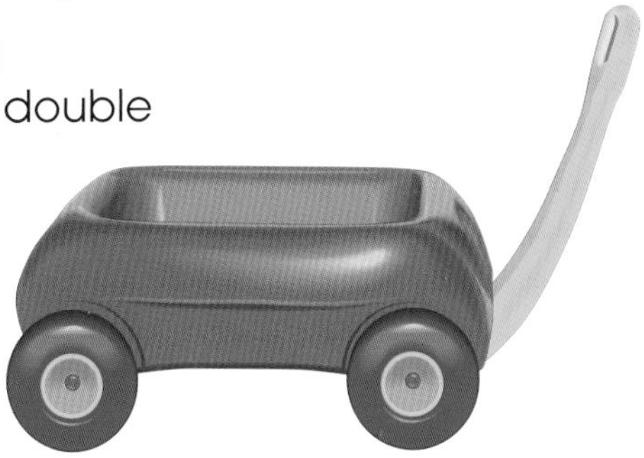
ball
ballon[M]

sandbox
bac[M] à sable[M]

in-ground swimming pool
piscine[F] creusée
garage
garage[M]
roof
toit[M]
chimney
cheminée[F]
window
fenêtre[F]
door
porte[F]
hedge
haie[F]

The bedroom
La chambre

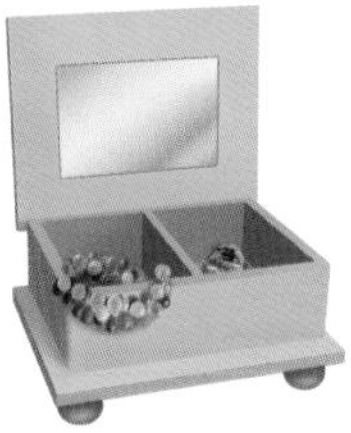

jewel box
coffret[M] à bijoux[M]

music box
boîte[F] à musique[F]

mobile
mobile[M]

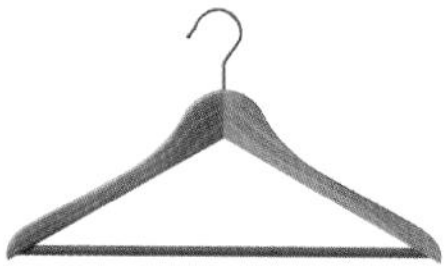

hanger
cintre[M]

changing table
table[F] à langer

alarm clock
réveil[M]

mirror
miroir[M]

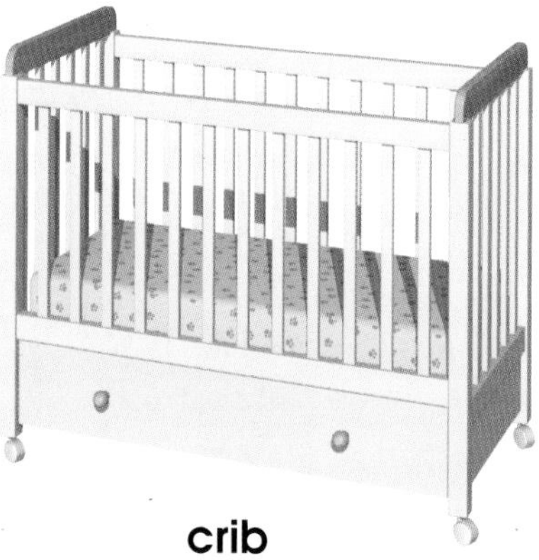

crib
lit[M] à barreaux[M]

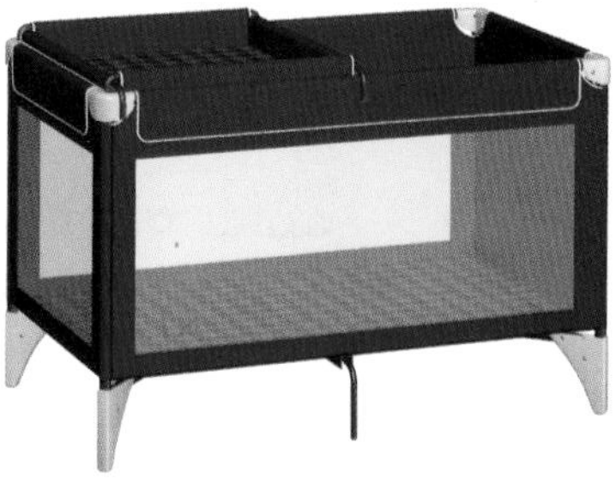

playpen
lit[M] pliant

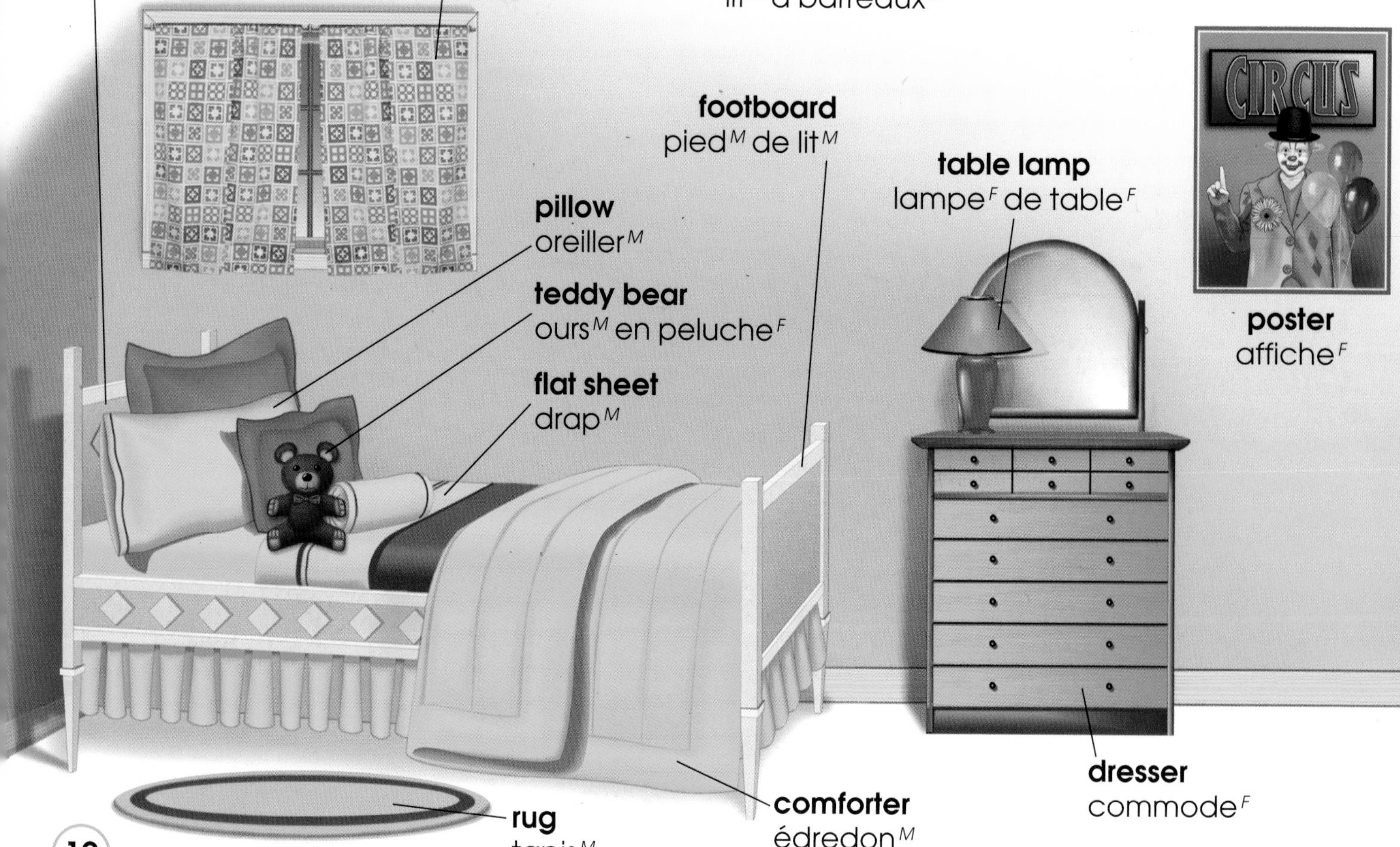

CD-radio-cassette player
radiocassette^F laser^M

cassette
cassette^F

ceiling fixture
plafonnier^M

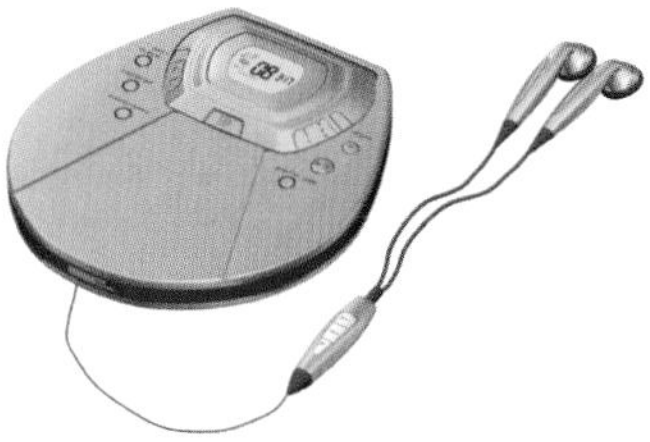

personal stereo
baladeur^M

compact disc
disque^M compact

chiffonier
chiffonnier^M

rocking chair
berceuse^F

linen chest
coffre^M

bedside table
table^F de chevet^M

wardrobe
armoire^F-penderie^F

coat hooks
patère^F

laundry basket
panier^M à linge^M

slipper
pantoufle^F

door
porte^F

The bathroom
La salle de bain

cotton applicators
coton^M-tige^F

bubble bath
bain^M moussant

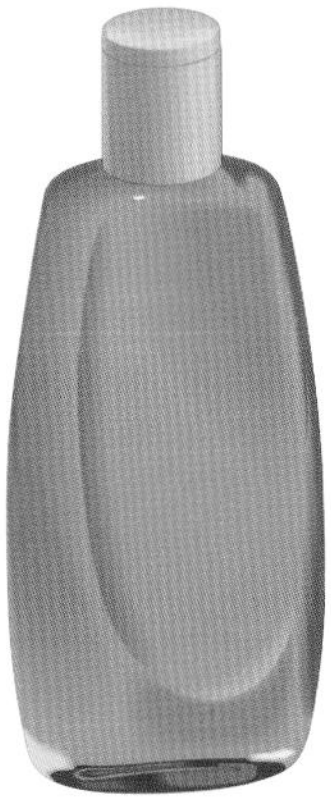

shampoo
shampooing^M

sponge
éponge^F

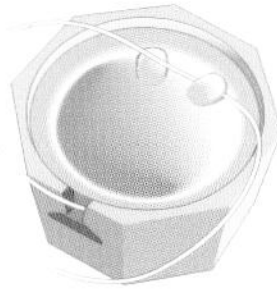

dental floss
fil^M dentaire

toothpaste
dentifrice^M

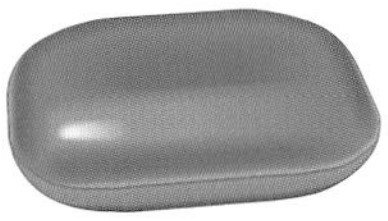

soap
savon^M

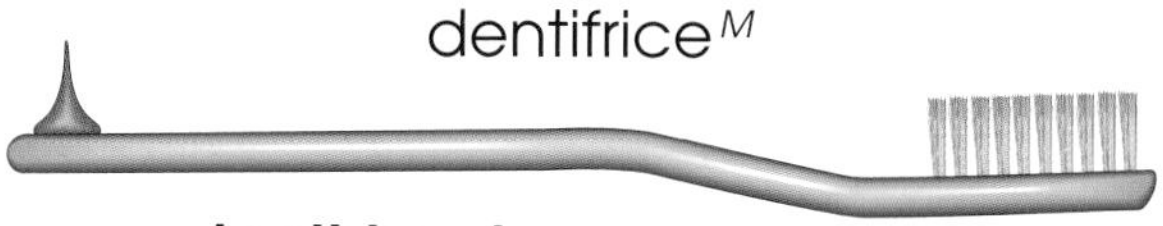

toothbrush
brosse^F à dents^F

adhesive bandage
pansement^M adhésif

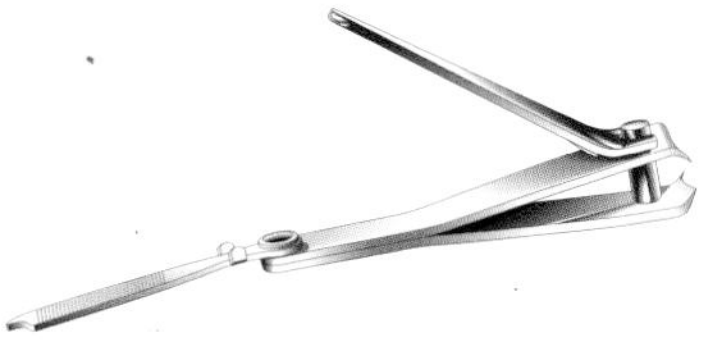

nail clippers
coupe-ongles^M

mouthwash
rince-bouche^M

tissues
papiers^M-mouchoirs^M

toilet paper
papier^M hygiénique

bathroom scale
pèse-personne^M

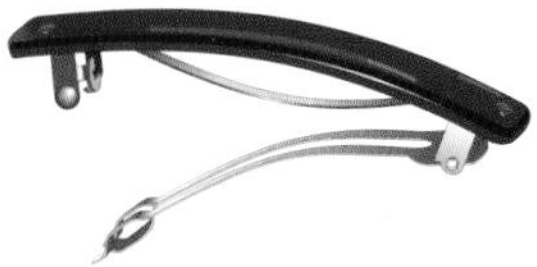

barrette
barrette[F]

bobby pin
pince[F] à cheveux[M]

blusher
fard[M] à joues[F]

nail enamel
vernis[M] à ongles[M]

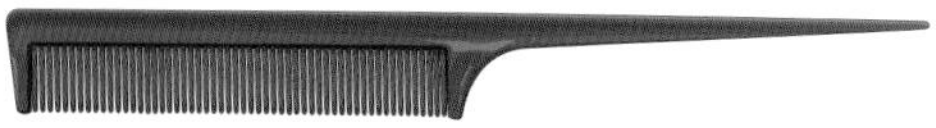

comb
peigne[M]

eyeshadow
ombre[F] à paupières[F]

perfume
parfum[M]

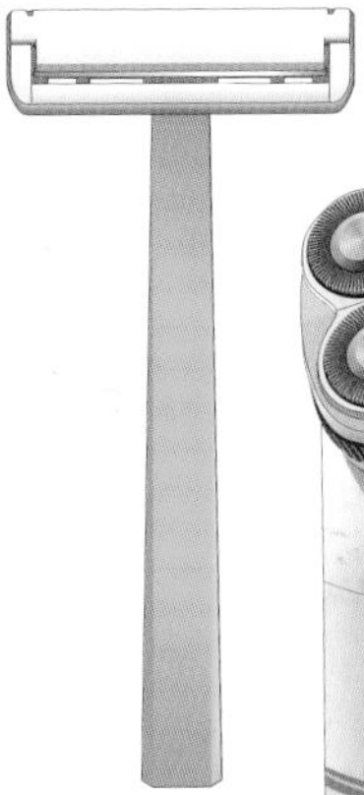

disposable razor
rasoir[M] jetable

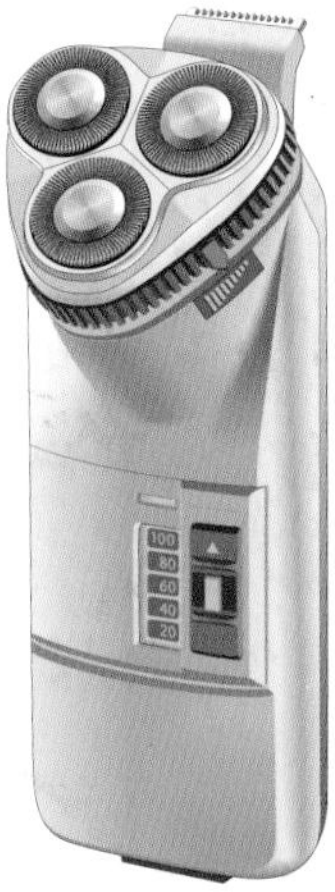

electric razor
rasoir[M] électrique

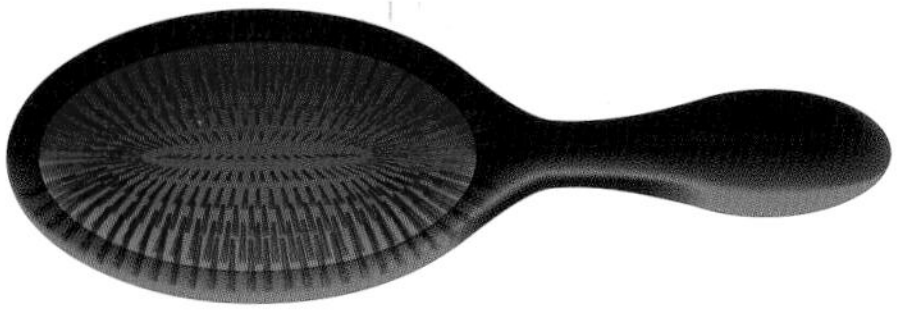

hairbrush
brosse[F]

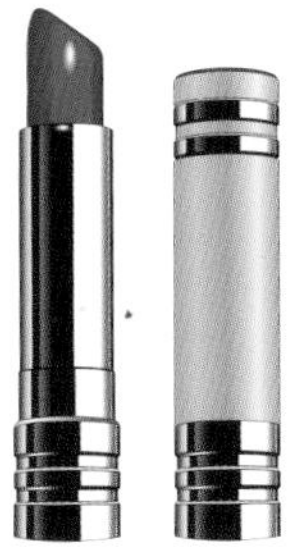

lipstick
rouge[M] à lèvres[F]

hair dryer
sèche-cheveux[M]

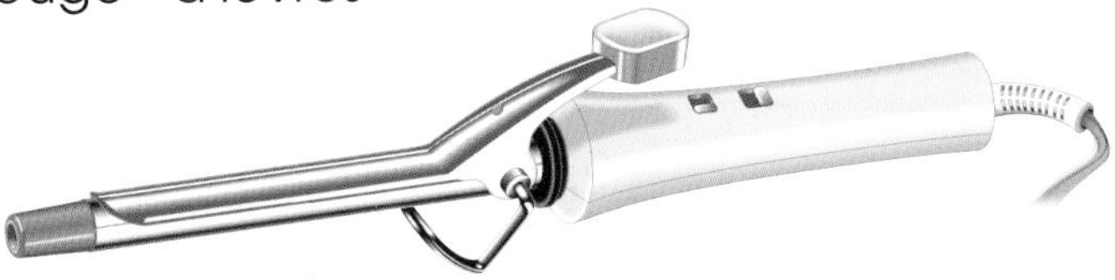

curling iron
fer[M] à friser

dryer
sécheuse[F]

washer
laveuse[F]

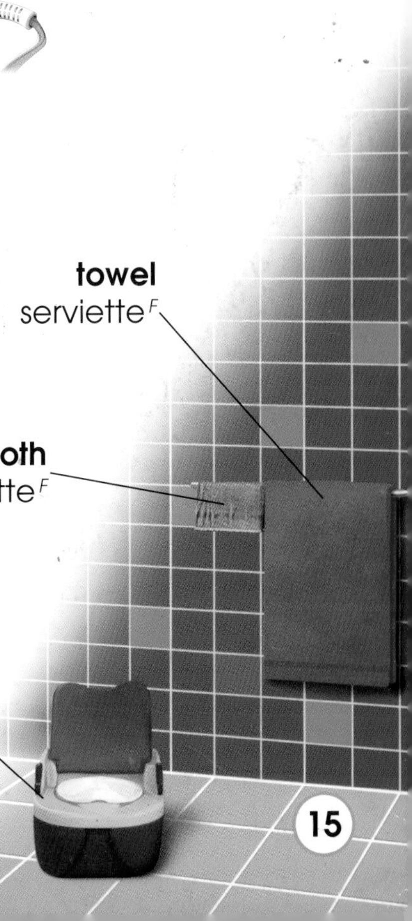

The living room
Le salon

fan
ventilateur^M

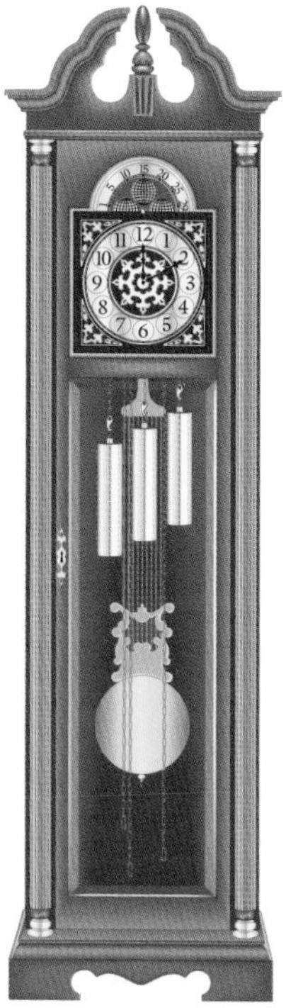

grandfather clock
horloge^F de parquet^M

armchair
fauteuil^M

ottoman
pouf^M

futon
futon^M

sofa bed
canapé^M convertible

folding chairs
chaises^F pliantes

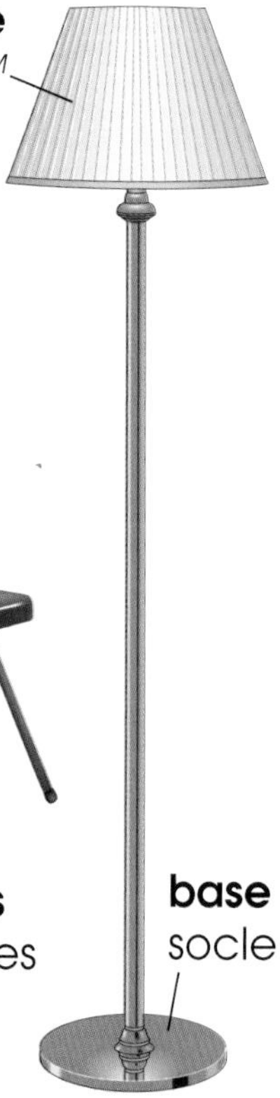

shade
abat-jour^M

base
socle^M

floor lamp
lampadaire^M

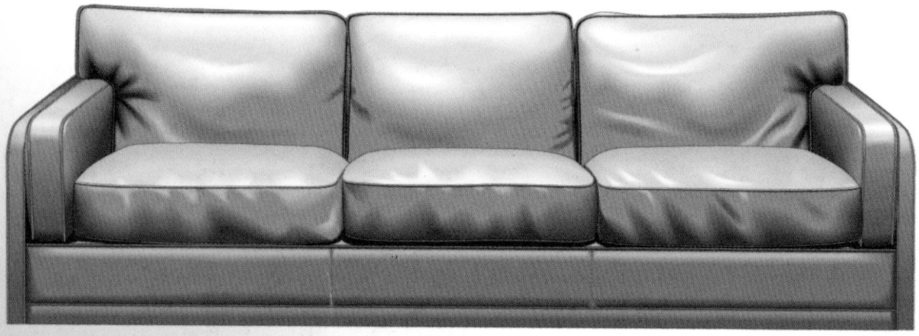

sofa
canapé^M

love seat
causeuse^F

cushion
coussin^M

table
table^F

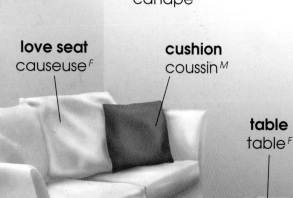

fireplace
foyer^M

television set
téléviseur^{M}

DVD player
lecteur^{M} de DVD^{M}

DVD
DVD^{M}

remote control
télécommande^{F}

videocassette
cassette^{F} vidéo

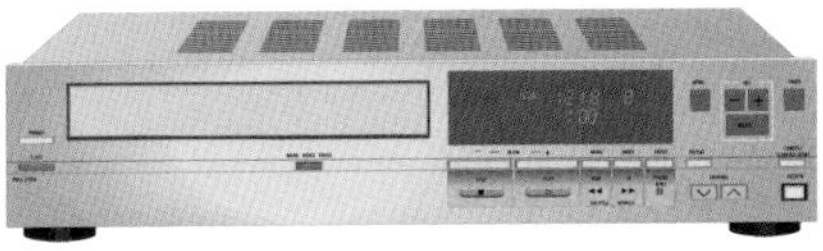

videocassette recorder (VCR)
magnétoscope^{M}

telephone
téléphone^{M}

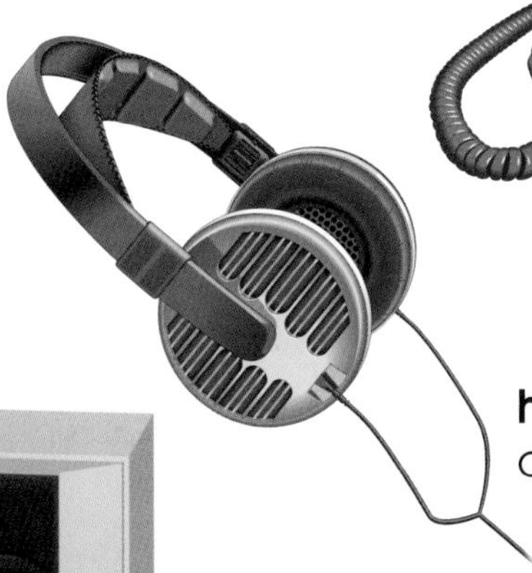

headphones
casque^{M} d'écoute^{F}

mini stereo sound system
minichaîne^{F} stéréo

compact disc player
lecteur^{M} de disque^{M} compact

cassette player
lecteur^{M} de cassette^{F}

speaker
haut-parleur^{M}

book
livre^{M}

bookcase
bibliothèque^{F}

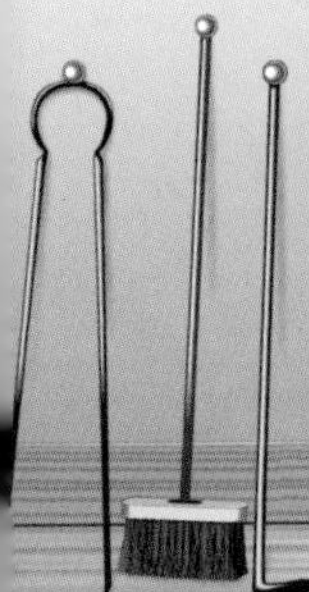

fire irons
accessoires^{M} de foyer^{M}

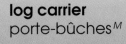

log carrier
porte-bûches^{M}

The playroom
La salle de jeux

drawing board
planche^F à dessiner

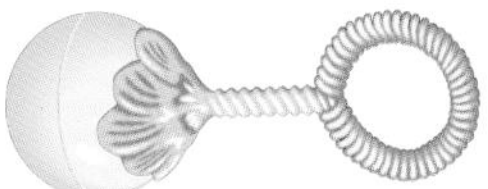

rattle
hochet^M

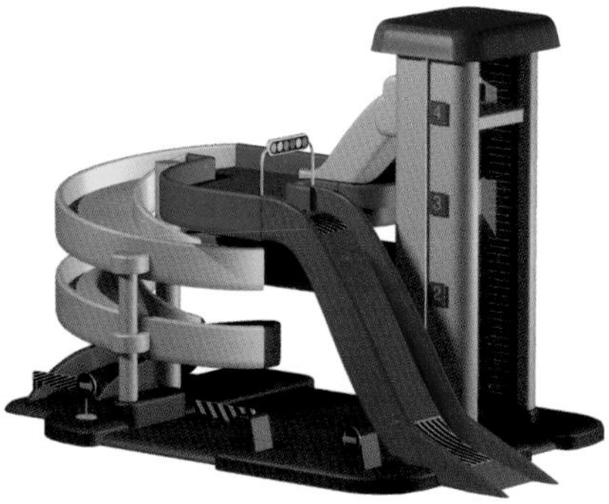

toy garage
garage^M

toy cars
petites voitures^F

modeling clay
pâte^F à modeler

assembly toy
personnage^M à assembler

toy train
train^M miniature

interlocking blocks
briques^F

rocking horse
cheval^M à bascule^F

walker
trotteur^M

doll
poupée^F

stroller
poussette^F

workbench
établi^M

spinning top
toupie^F

stackable rings
anneaux^M à empiler

blocks
cubes^M

peg puzzle
casse-tête^M

felt tip pen
feutre^{M}

brush
pinceau^{M}

adhesive tape
ruban^{M} adhésif

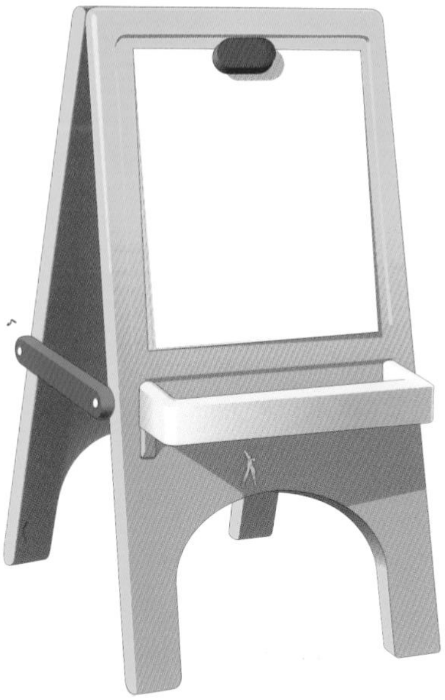

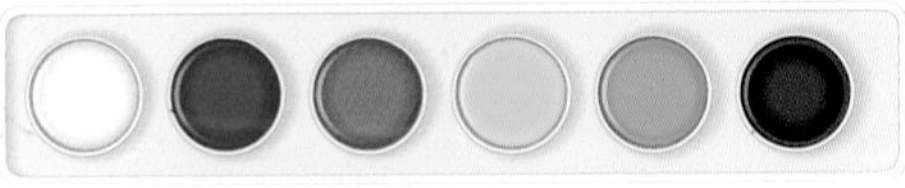

watercolor paints
pastilles^{F} d'aquarelle^{F}

glue stick
bâtonnet^{M} de colle^{F}

scissors
ciseaux^{M}

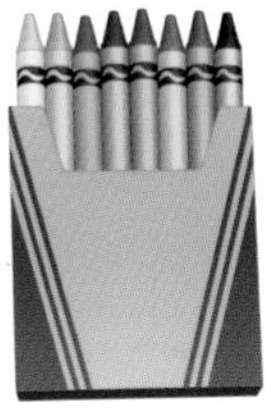

crayons
crayons^{M} de cire^{F}

easel
chevalet^{M}

colored pencils
crayons^{M} de couleur^{F}

memo pad
bloc^{M}-notes^{F}

cards
cartes^{F}

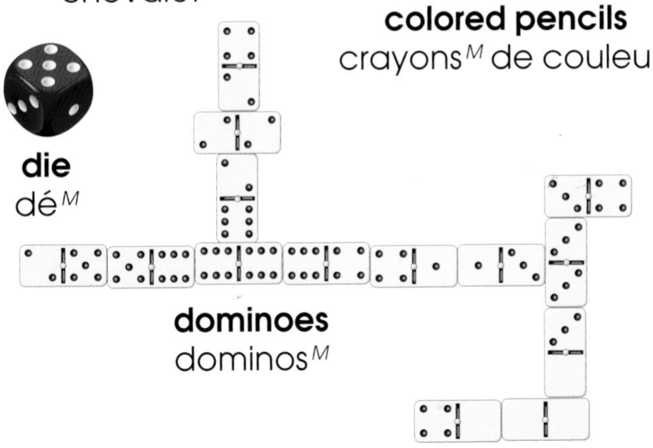

die
dé^{M}

dominoes
dominos^{M}

darts
jeu^{M} de fléchettes^{F}

monitor
écran^{M}

game console
console^{F} de jeu^{M}

controller
manette^{F} de jeu^{M}

video entertainment system
système^{M} de jeux^{M} vidéo

soccer table
baby-foot^{M}

The kitchen
La cuisine

toaster
grille-pain^M

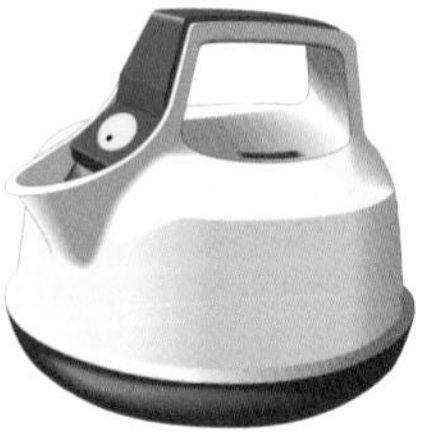

kettle
bouilloire^F

coffeemaker
cafetière^F

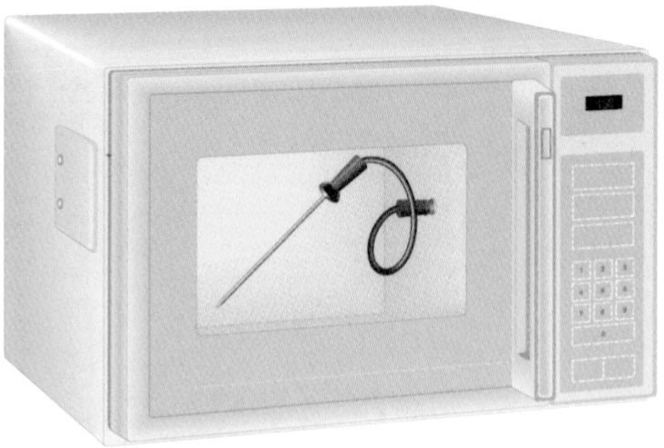

microwave oven
four^M à micro-ondes^F

colander
passoire^F

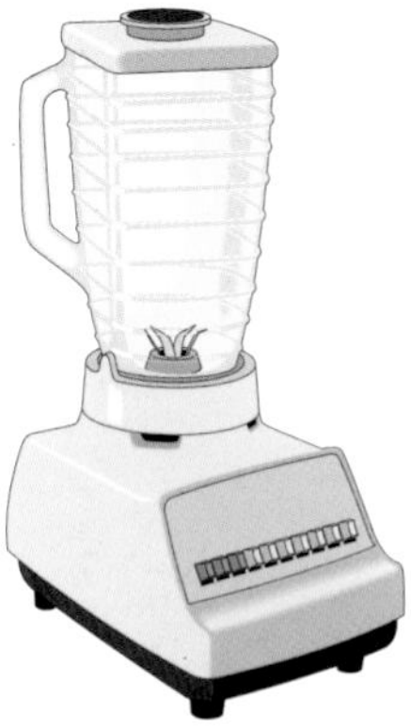

blender
mélangeur^M

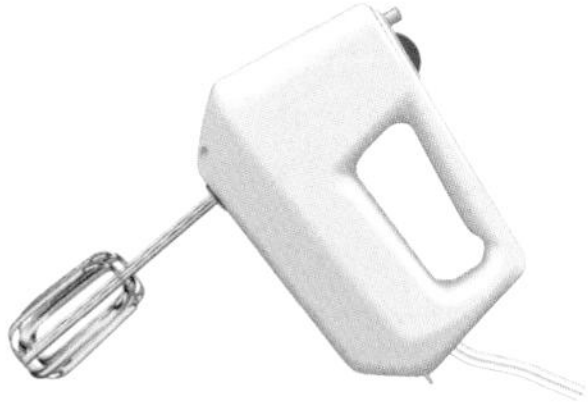

hand mixer
batteur^M à main^F

salad spinner
essoreuse^F à salade^F

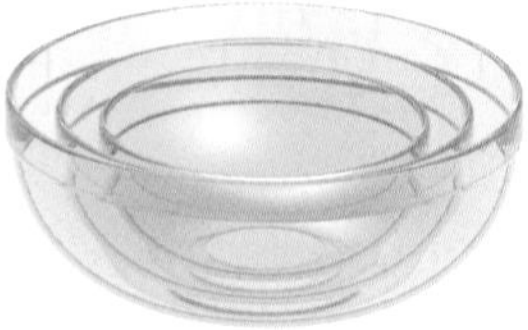

mixing bowls
bols^M à mélanger

oven mitt
mitaine^F isolante

apron
tablier^M

freezer
congélateur^M

cabinet
armoire^F

sink
évier^M

refrigerator
réfrigérateur^M

dishwasher
lave-vaisselle^M

drawer
tiroir^M

funnel
entonnoir[M]

kitchen timer
minuteur[M]

scouring pad
éponge[F] à récurer

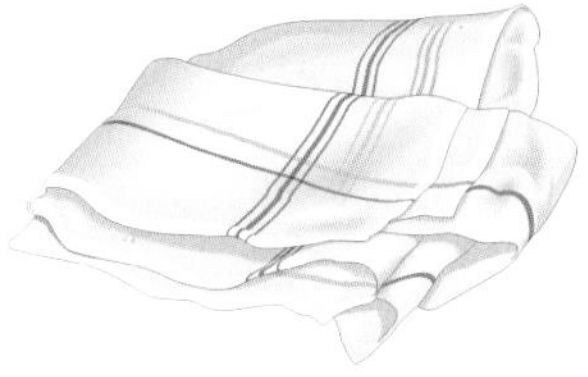

tea towel
torchon[M]

measuring spoons
cuillers[F] doseuses

measuring cup
tasse[F] à mesurer

corkscrew
tire-bouchon[M]

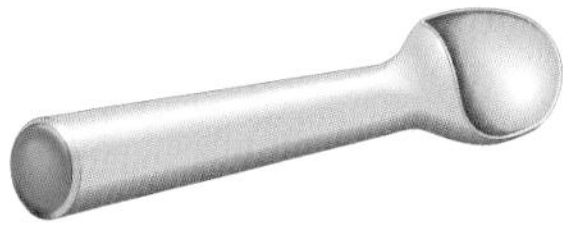

ice-cream scoop
cuiller[F] à crème[F] glacée

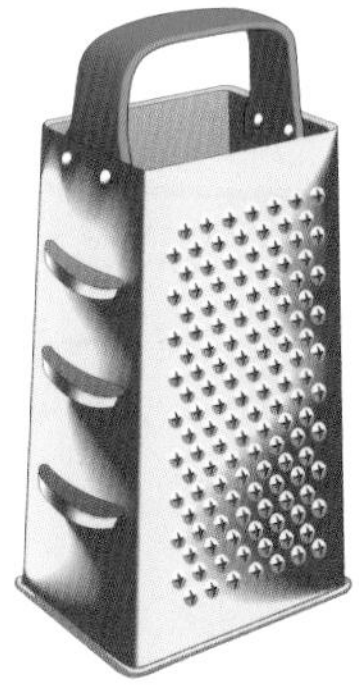

grater
râpe[F]

cookie cutters
emporte-pièces[M]

peeler
éplucheur[M]

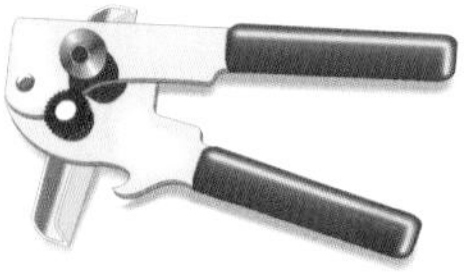

can opener
ouvre-boîtes[M]

kitchen knife
couteau[M] de cuisine[F]

citrus juicer
presse-agrumes[M]

cutting board
planche[F] à découper

pie pan
moule[M] à tarte[F]

rolling pin
rouleau[M] à pâtisserie[F]

electric range
cuisinière[F] électrique

frying pan
poêle[F] à frire

saucepan
casserole[F]

stock pot
marmite[F]

baking sheet
plaque[F] à pâtisserie[F]

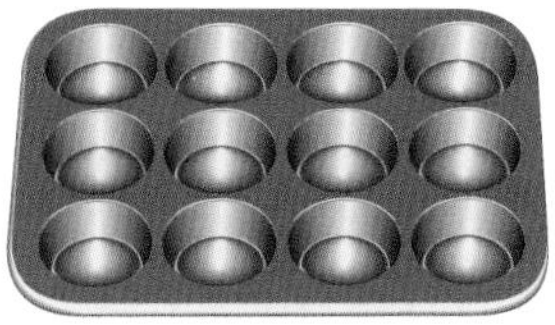

muffin pan
moule[M] à muffins[M]

The meal
Le repas

spouted cup
gobelet^{M} à bec^{M}

cup
tasse^{F}

wineglass
verre^{M} à vin^{M}

small decanter
carafon^{M}

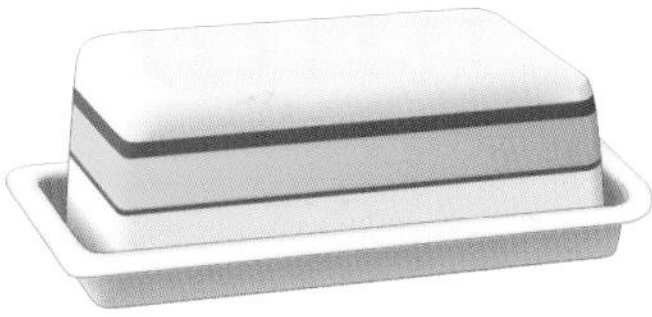

butter dish
beurrier^{M}

teapot
théière^{F}

sugar bowl
sucrier^{M}

creamer
crémier^{M}

ramekin
ramequin^{M}

water pitcher
pichet^{M}

salad bowl
saladier^{M}

soup bowl
bol^{M}

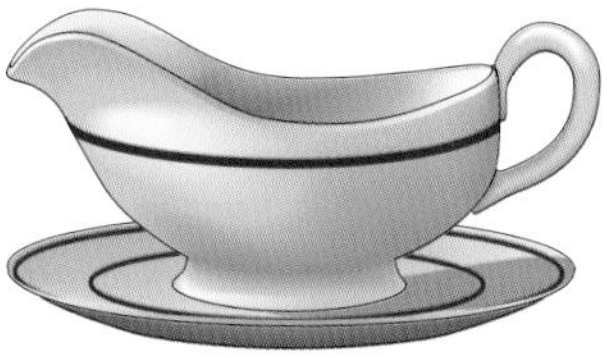

gravy boat
saucière^{F}

soup tureen
soupière^{F}

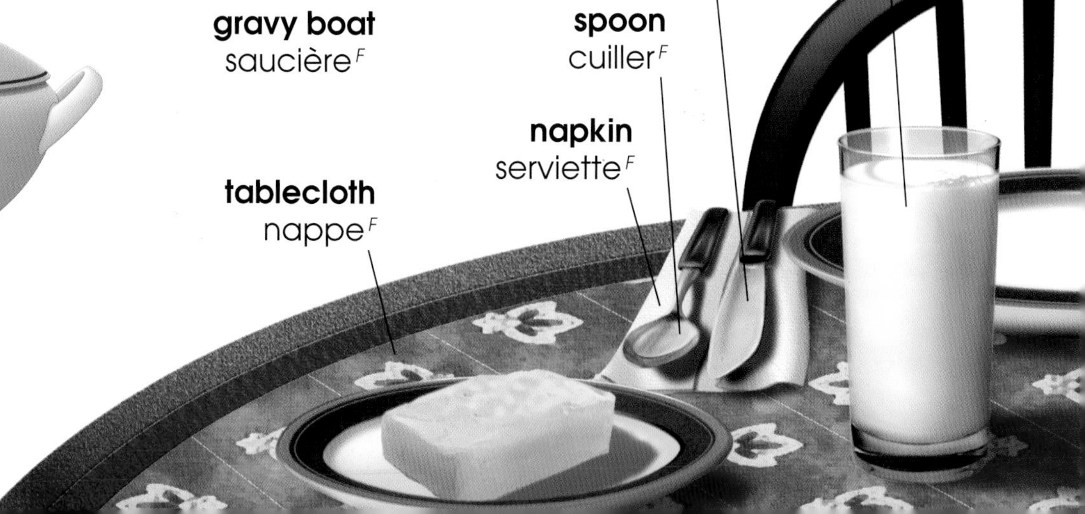

glass
verre^{M}

knife
couteau^{M}

spoon
cuiller^{F}

napkin
serviette^{F}

tablecloth
nappe^{F}

flour
farine^F

sandwich
sandwich^M

salad
salade^F

steak
steak^M

sugar
sucre^M

pizza
pizza^F

turkey
dinde^F

fish
poisson^M

brown sugar
cassonade^F

stew
ragoût^M

cereal
céréales^F

spaghetti
spaghetti^M

maple syrup
sirop^M d'érable^M

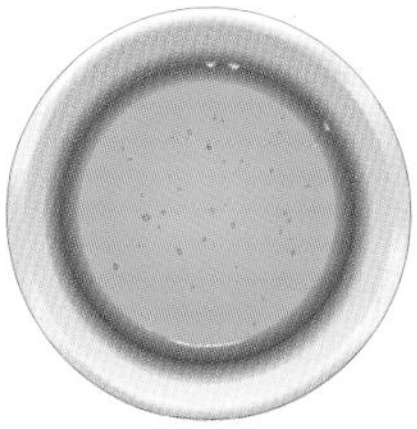

honey
miel^M

cookies
biscuits^M

ice cream
crème^F glacée

pie
tarte^F

bun
brioche^F

cake
gâteau^M

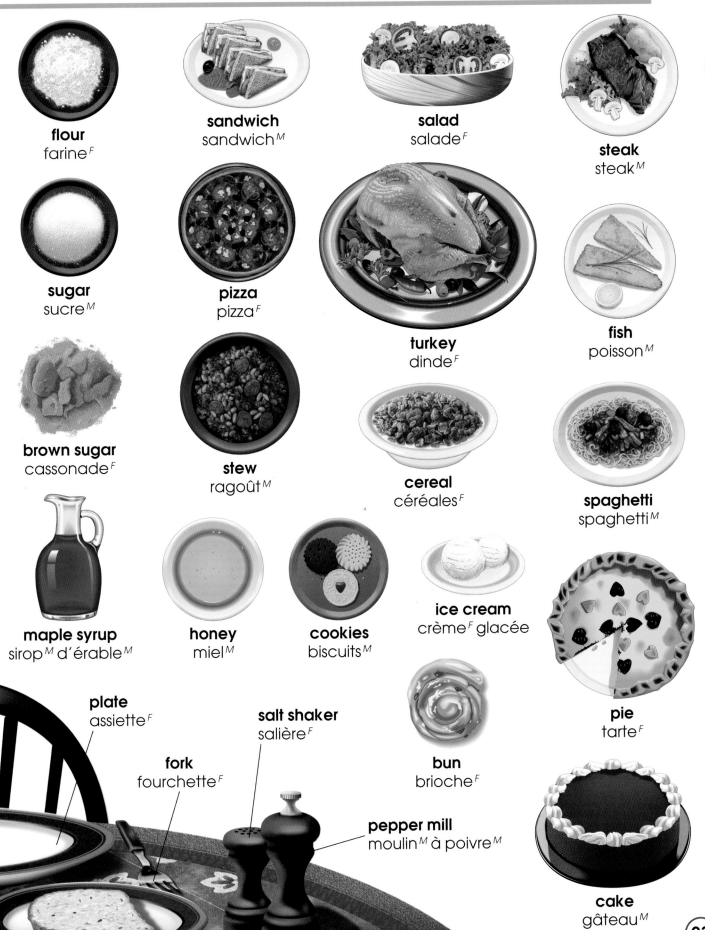

Vegetables
Le potager et les légumes

asparagus
asperge[F]

artichoke
artichaut[M]

rhubarb
rhubarbe[F]

lettuce
laitue[F]

cauliflower
chou[M]-fleur[F]

spinach
épinard[M]

cabbage
chou[M]

fennel
fenouil[M]

broccoli
brocoli[M]

celery
céleri[M]

brussels sprouts
choux[M] de Bruxelles

potatoes
pommes[F] de terre[F]

carrot
carotte[F]

parsnip
panais[M]

beet
betterave[F]

turnip
navet[M]

radish
radis[M]

rutabaga
rutabaga[M]

sweet potato
patate[F]

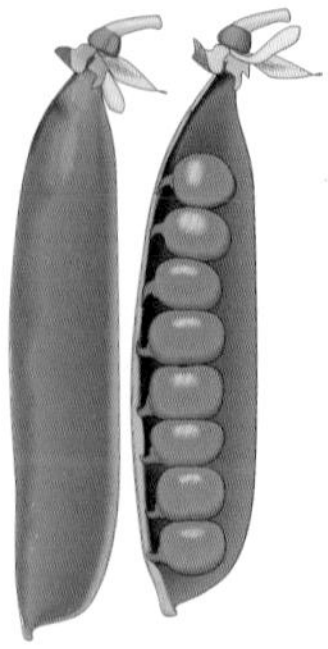

green peas
petits pois^M

bean
haricot^M

chives
ciboulette^F

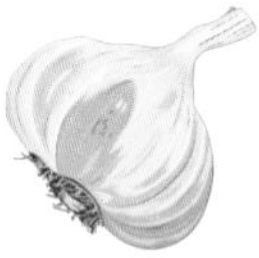

garlic
ail^M

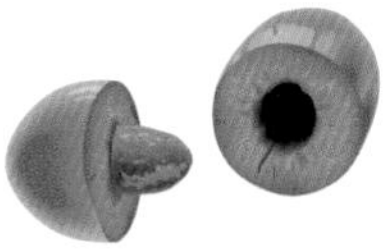

olives
olives^F

tomato
tomate^F

avocado
avocat^M

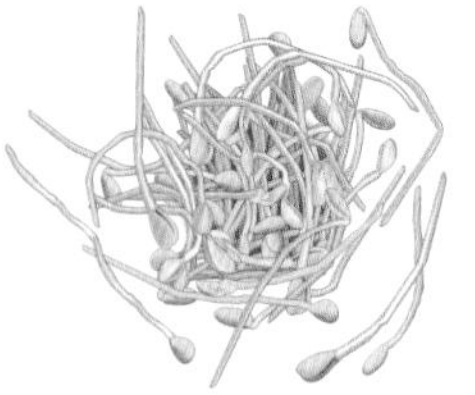

soybean sprouts
germes^M de soja^M

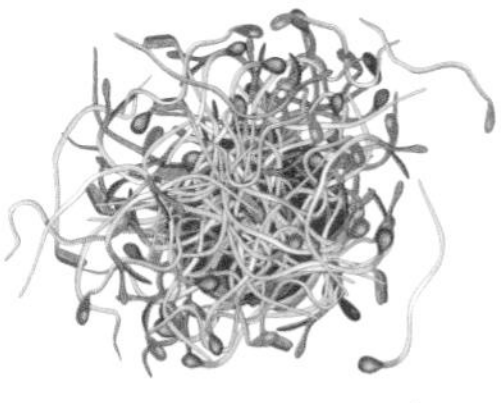

alfalfa sprouts
luzerne^F

gherkin
cornichon^M

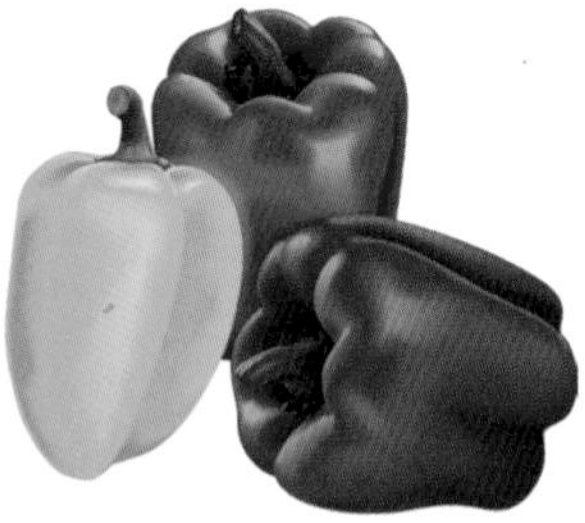

sweet pepper
poivron^M

cucumber
concombre^M

zucchini
courgette^F

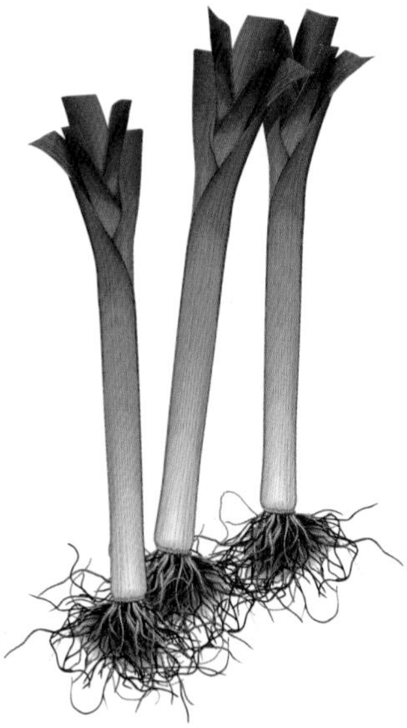

leeks
poireaux^M

onion
oignon^M

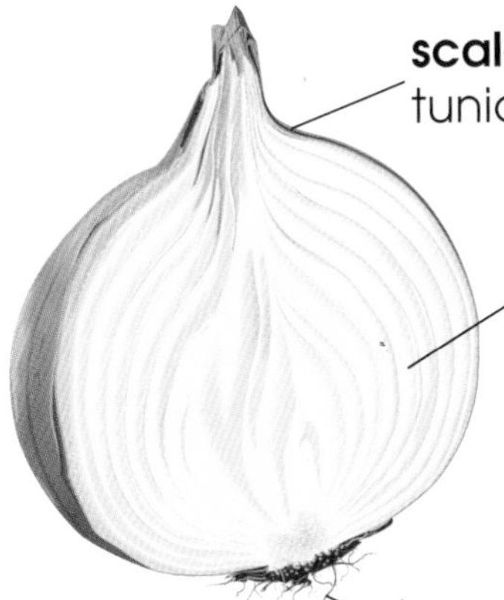

eggplant
aubergine^F

spaghetti squash
courge^F spaghetti^M

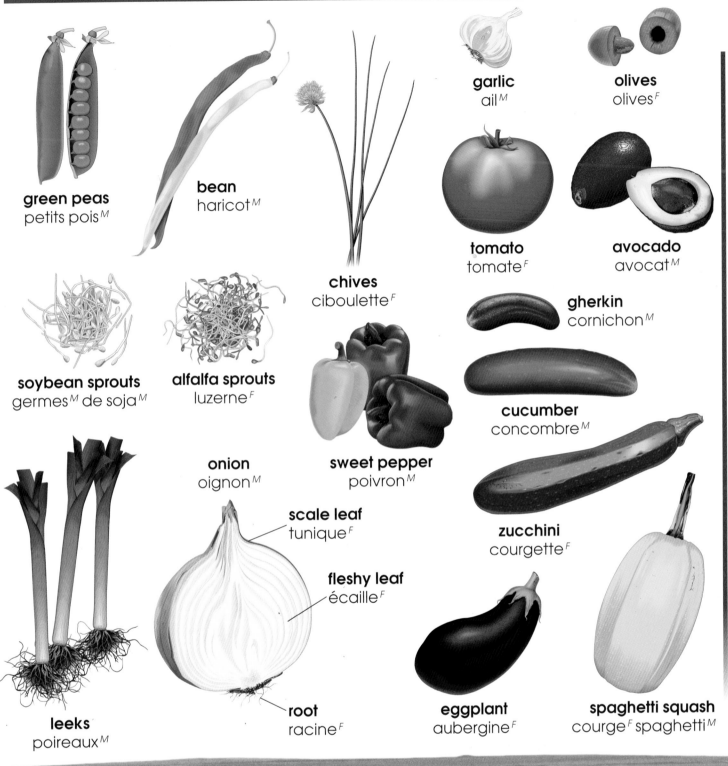

Fruits
Les fruits

pear
poire^F

banana
banane^F

lime
lime^F

lemon
citron^M

section of an apple
coupe^F d'une pomme^F

stem
queue^F

skin
peau^F

seed
pépin^M

nectarine
nectarine^F

peach
pêche^F

muskmelon
melon^M brodé

grapefruit
pamplemousse^M

honeydew melon
melon^M miel^M

apricot
abricot^M

plums
prunes^F

orange
orange^F

apple
pomme^F

strawberries
fraises^F

blueberries
bleuets^M

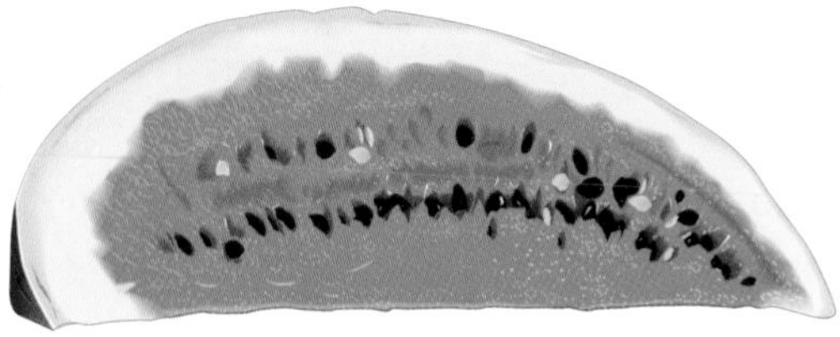

watermelon
melon^M d'eau^F

pomegranate
grenade^F

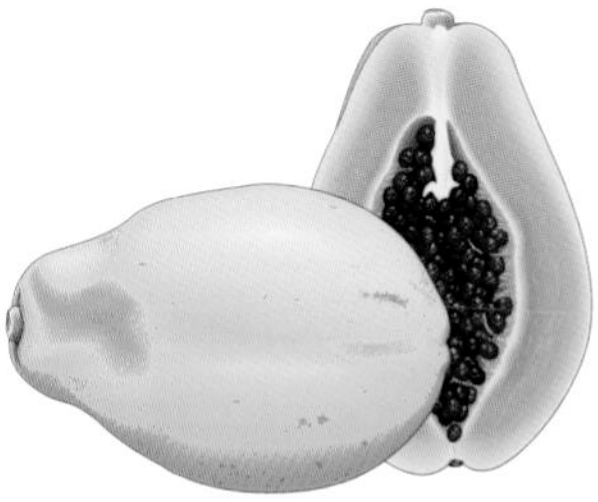

papaya
papaye^F

pineapple
ananas^M

raspberries
framboises^F

passion fruit
fruit^M de la Passion^F

carambola
carambole^F

kiwi
kiwi^M

mango
mangue^F

cranberry
canneberge^F

grapes
raisins^M

fig
figue^F

black currants
cassis^M

cherries
cerises^F

currant
gadelle^F

blackberries
mûres^F

prune
pruneau^M

raisin
raisin^M sec

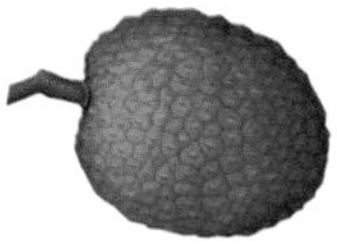

litchi
litchi^M

section of an orange
coupe^F d'une orange^F

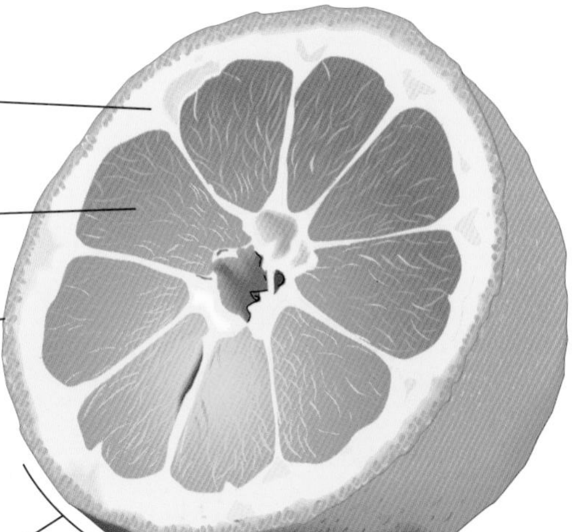

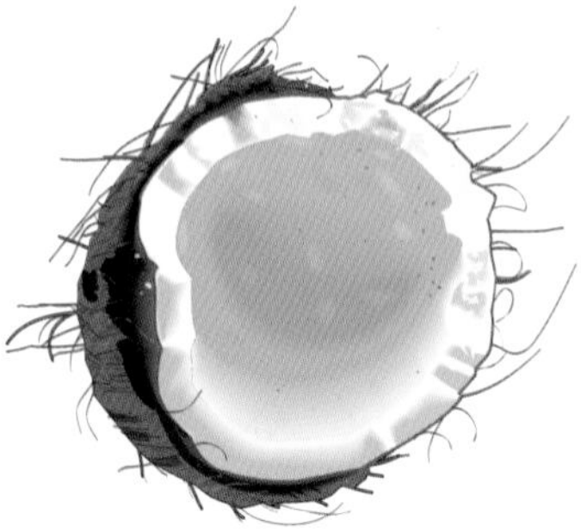

coconut
noix^F de coco^M

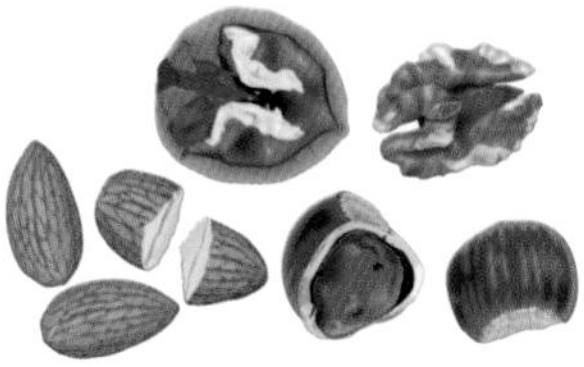

nuts
noix^F

The supermarket
L'épicerie

pasta
pâtes[F] alimentaires

tortillas
tortillas[F]

pita bread
pain[M] pita

white bread
pain[M] blanc

baguette
baguette[F]

bagel
bagel[M]

croissant
croissant[M]

rice
riz[M]

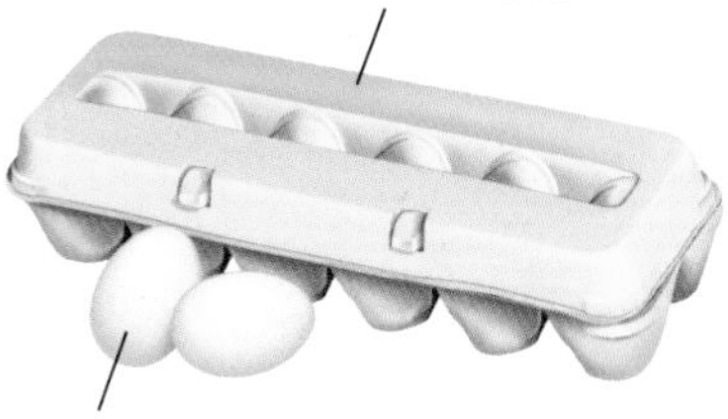

egg carton
boîte[F] à œufs[M]

egg
œuf[M]

cheese
fromages[M]

milk carton
berlingot[M] de lait[M]

ice cream cup
pot[M] de crème[F] glacée

yogurt
pot[M] de yogourt[M]

butter
beurre[M]

baby food
petits pots[M]

freezer bag
sac[M] de congélation[F]

spices
épices[F]

bag of cookies
sac[M] de biscuits[M]

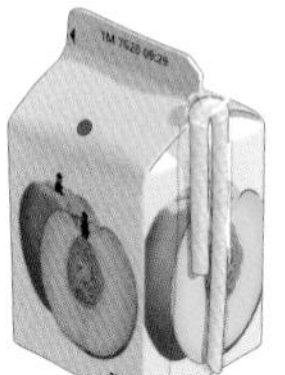

fruit juice
jus[M] de fruits[M]

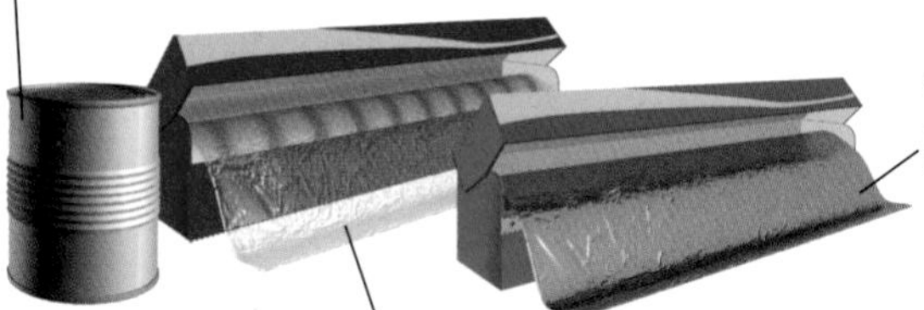

food can
boîte[F] de conserve[F]

aluminum foil
papier[M] aluminium[M]

plastic film (cellophane)
pellicule[F] plastique

cash register
caisse[F] enregistreuse

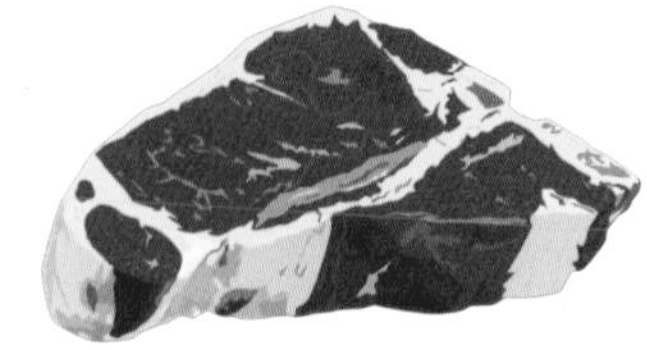

steak
bifteck^{M}

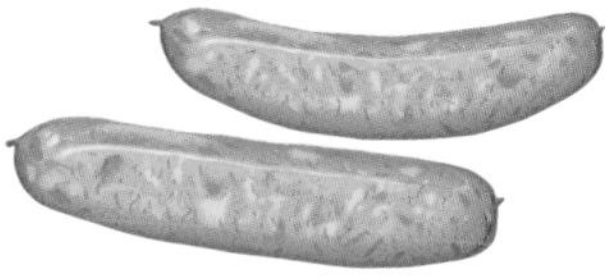

sausage
saucisse^{F}

lobster
homard^{M}

chicken
poulet^{M}

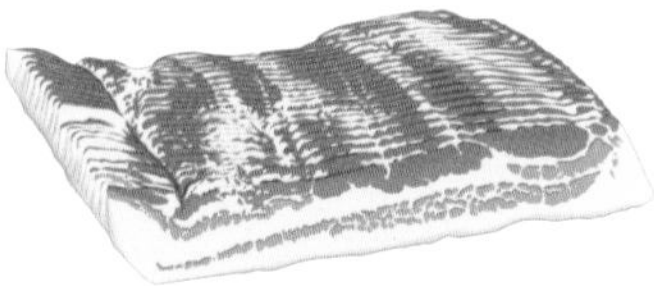

bacon
bacon^{M}

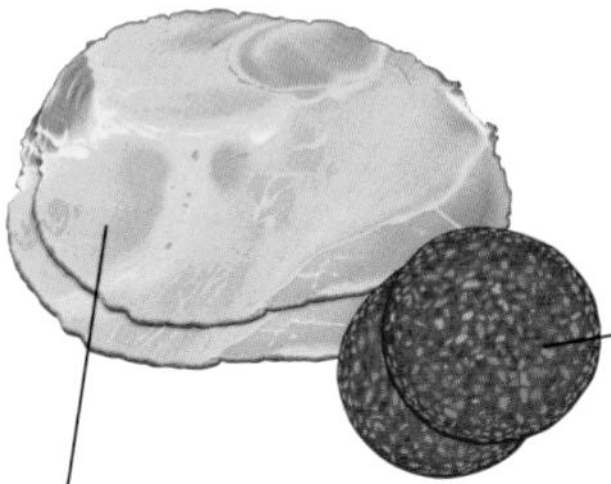

salami
salami^{M}

cooked ham
jambon^{M} cuit

chocolate bar
tablette^{F} de chocolat^{M}

candies
bonbons^{M}

salmon
saumon^{M}

mussel
moule^{F}

oyster
huître^{F}

counter
comptoir^{M} vitré

ketchup
ketchup^{M}

wine vinegar
vinaigre^{M} de vin^{M}

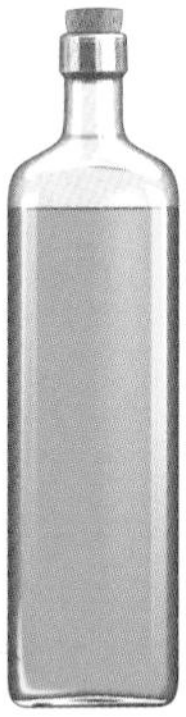

olive oil
huile^{F} d'olive^{F}

shopping cart
chariot^{M}

shopping basket
panier^{M}

Familiar animals
Les animaux familiers

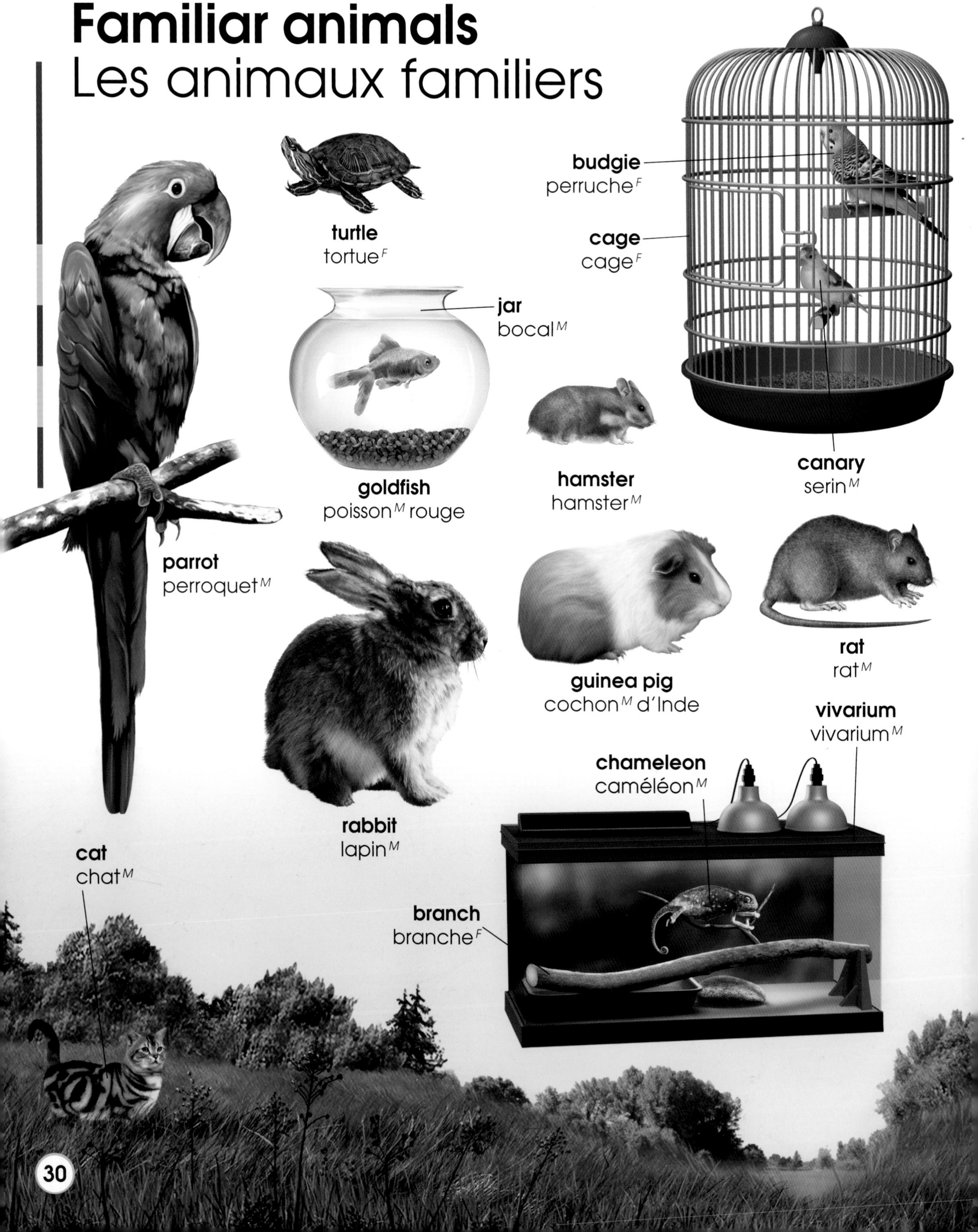

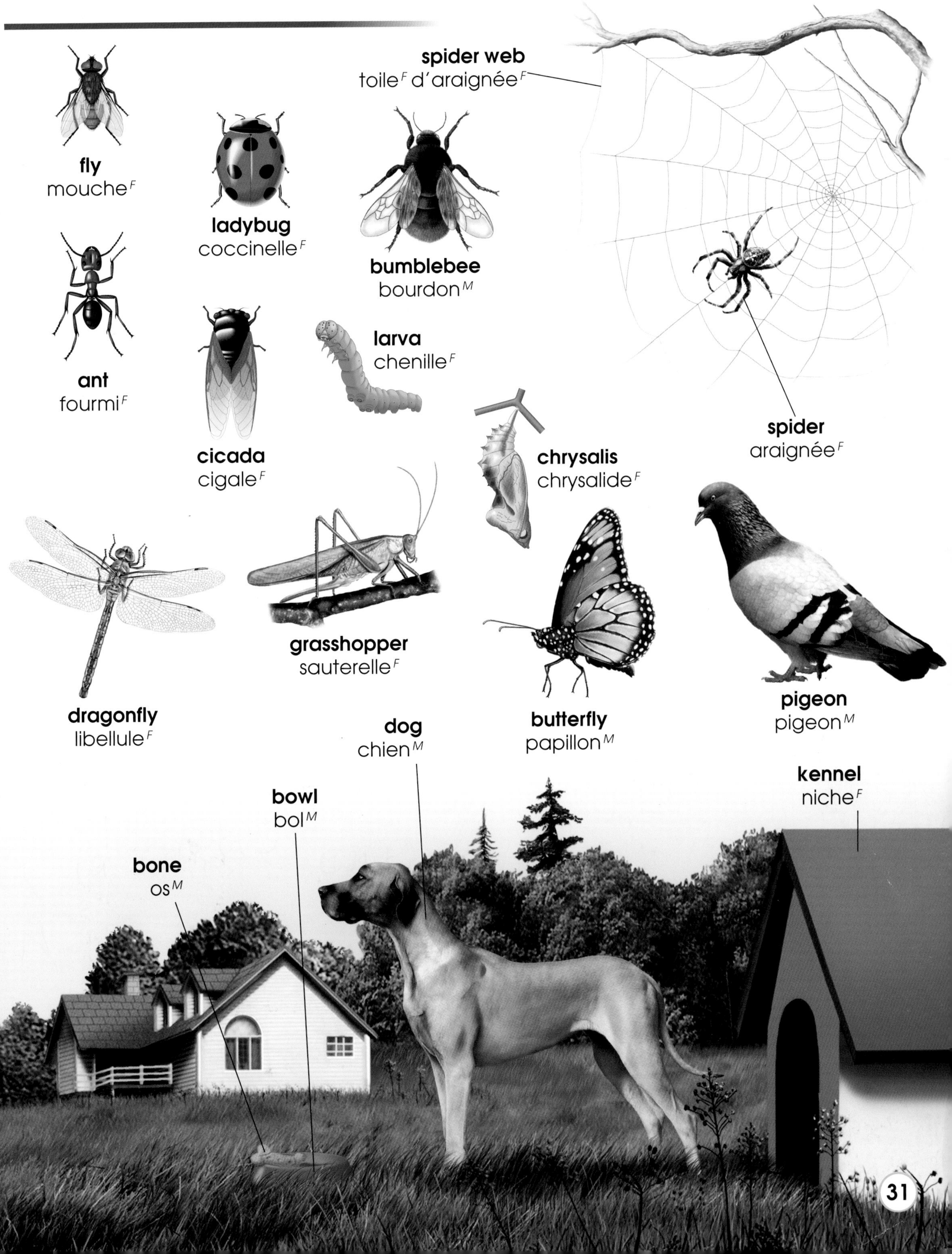
spider web
toile^{F} d'araignée^{F}
fly
mouche^{F}
ladybug
coccinelle^{F}
bumblebee
bourdon^{M}
ant
fourmi^{F}
larva
chenille^{F}
cicada
cigale^{F}
chrysalis
chrysalide^{F}
spider
araignée^{F}
grasshopper
sauterelle^{F}
dragonfly
libellule^{F}
butterfly
papillon^{M}
pigeon
pigeon^{M}
dog
chien^{M}
kennel
niche^{F}
bowl
bol^{M}
bone
os^{M}

The farm
La ferme

quail
caille^F

ostrich
autruche^F

turkey
dindon^M

duck
canard^M

goose
oie^F

chick
poussin^M

hen
poule^F

goat
chèvre^F

sheep
mouton^M

horse
cheval^M

horseshoe
fer^M à cheval^M

donkey
âne^M

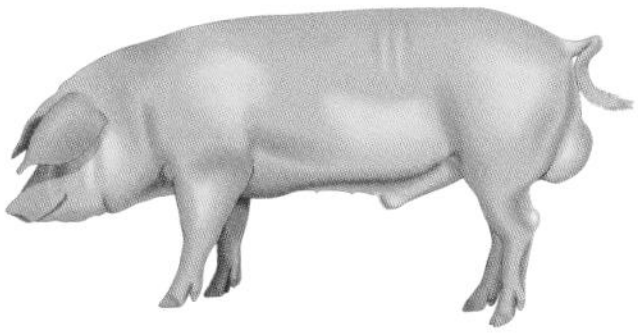

pig
porc^M

corn
maïs ^{M}

wheat
blé ^{M}

millet
millet ^{M}

barley
orge ^{F}

oats
avoine ^{F}

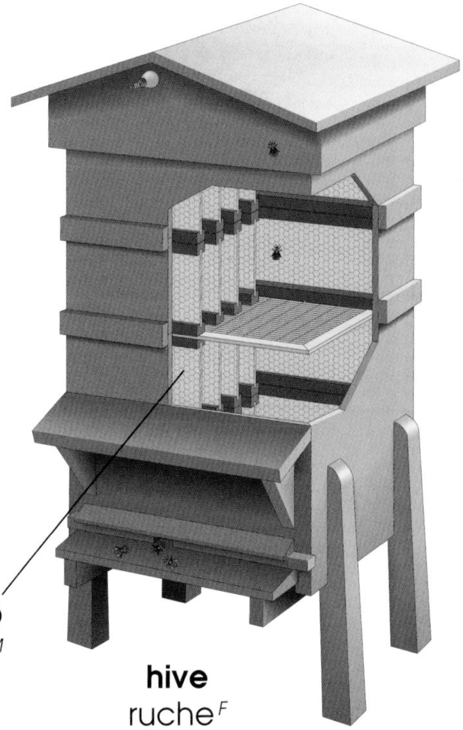

honeycomb
rayon ^{M} de miel ^{M}

hive
ruche ^{F}

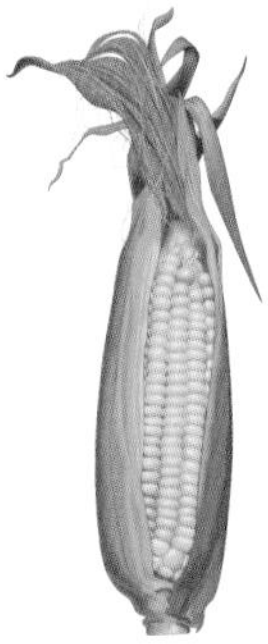

corncob
épi ^{M} de maïs ^{M}

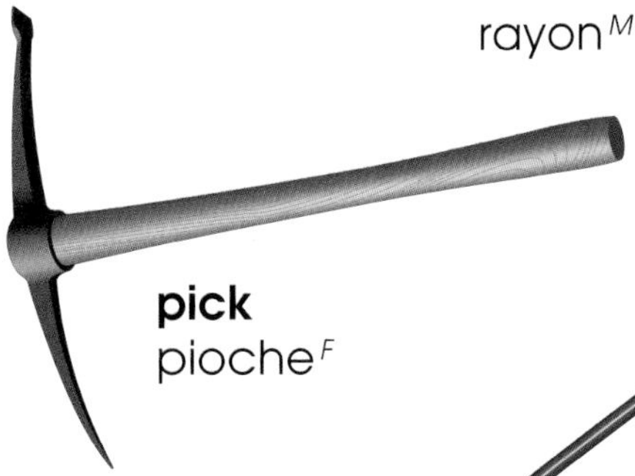

pick
pioche ^{F}

honeybee
abeille ^{F}

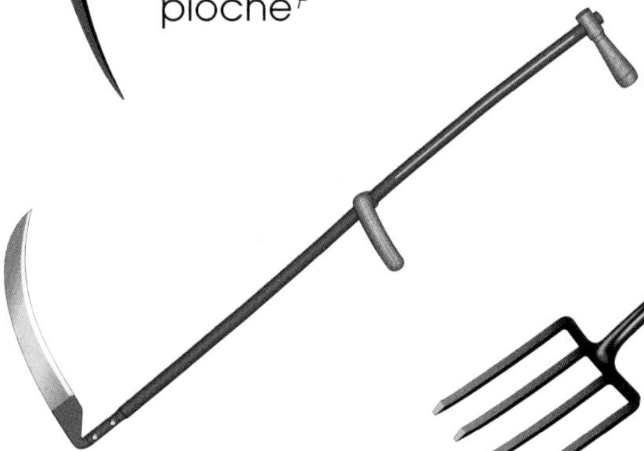

scythe
faux ^{F}

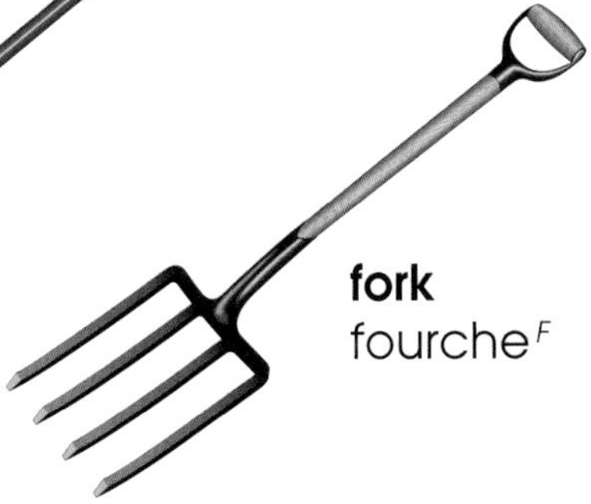

fork
fourche ^{F}

calf
veau ^{M}

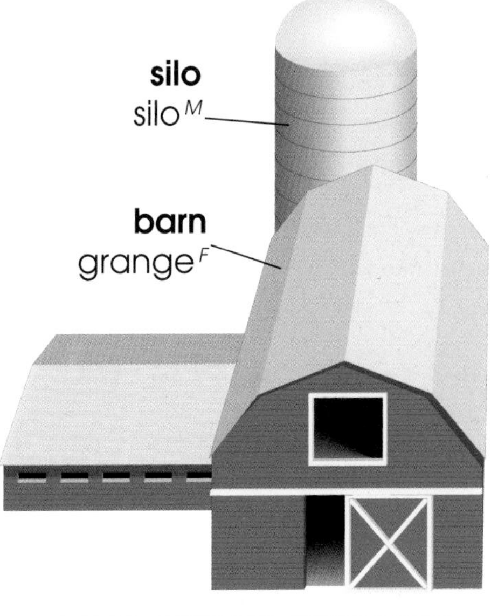

silo
silo ^{M}

barn
grange ^{F}

ox
bœuf ^{M}

The forest
La forêt

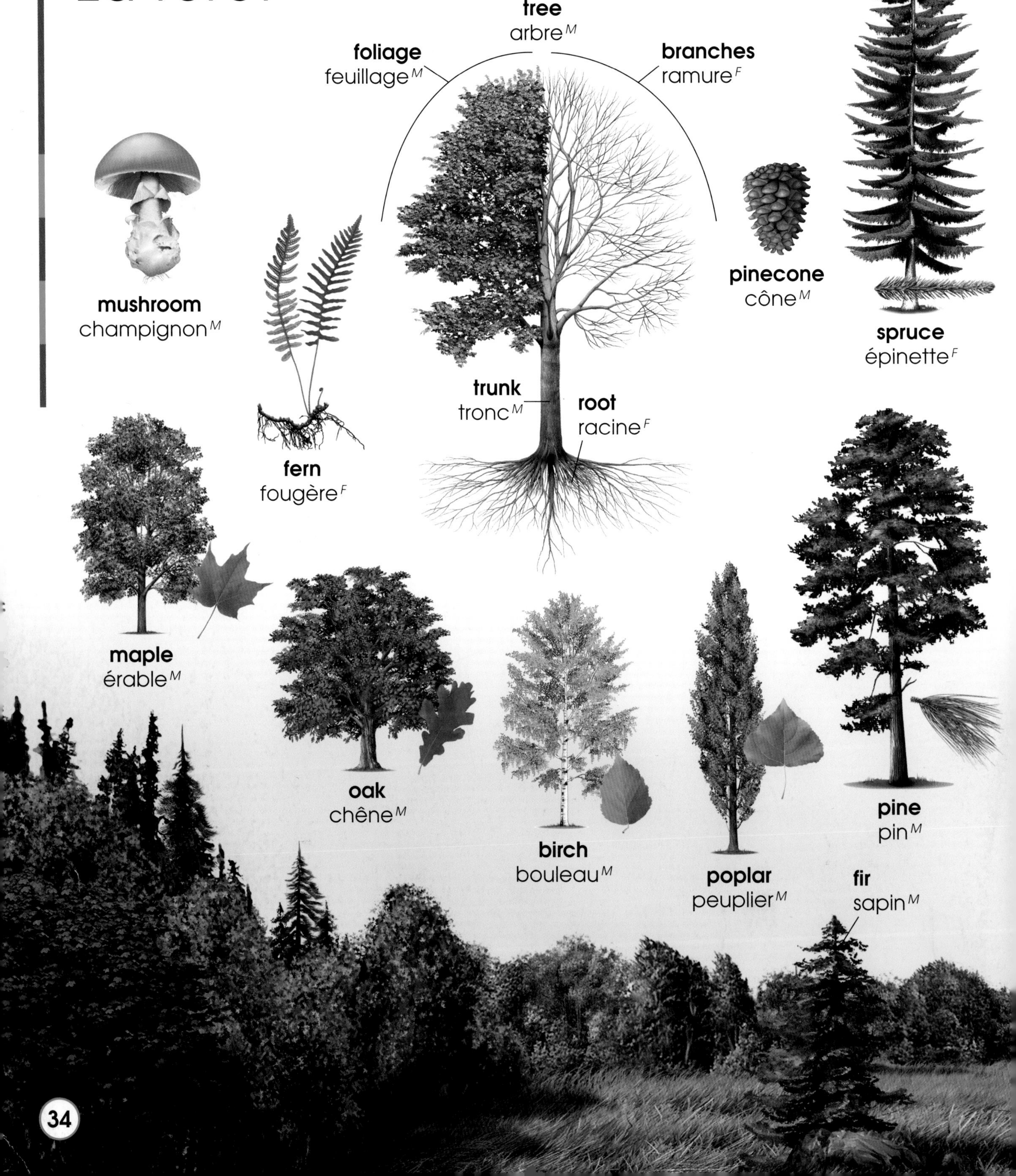

tree
arbre[M]
foliage
feuillage[M]
branches
ramure[F]
mushroom
champignon[M]
fern
fougère[F]
trunk
tronc[M]
root
racine[F]
pinecone
cône[M]
spruce
épinette[F]
maple
érable[M]
oak
chêne[M]
birch
bouleau[M]
poplar
peuplier[M]
pine
pin[M]
fir
sapin[M]

sparrow
moineau^M

goldfinch
chardonneret^M

jay
geai^M

owl
hibou^M

falcon
faucon^M

woodpecker
pic^M

robin
rouge-gorge^M

field mouse
mulot^M

frog
grenouille^F

skunk
moufette^F

chipmunk
tamia^M

porcupine
porc-épic^M

squirrel
écureuil^M

snake
couleuvre^F

hare
lièvre^M

wolf
loup^M

beaver
castor^M

moose
orignal^M

bear
ours^M

The desert and the savanna
Le désert et la savane

tick
tique^{F}

tarantula
mygale^{F}

jerboa
gerboise^{F}

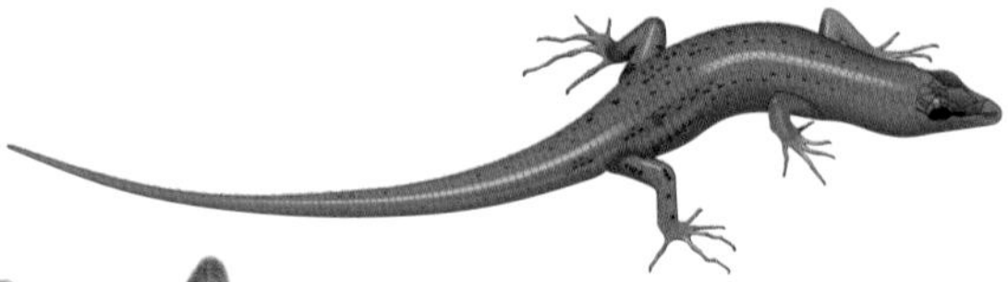

lizard
lézard^{M}

scorpion
scorpion^{M}

claw
pince^{F}

vulture
vautour^{M}

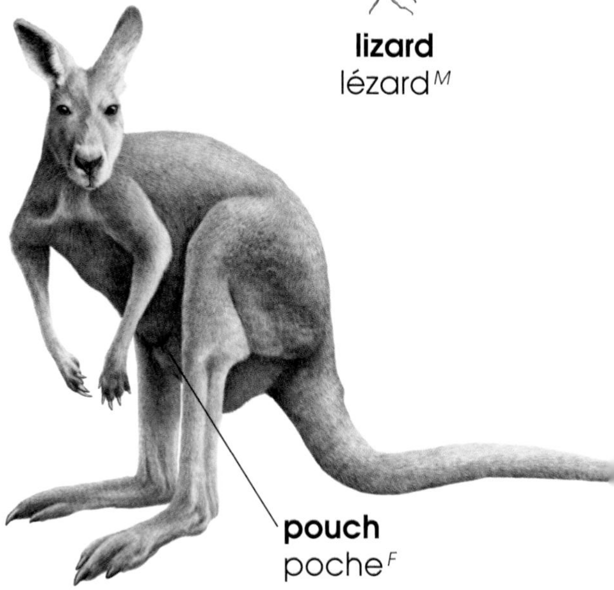

pouch
poche^{F}

kangaroo
kangourou^{M}

rattlesnake
serpent^{M} à sonnette^{F}

dromedary camel
dromadaire^{M}

bactrian camel
chameau^{M}

fennec
fennec^{M}

giraffe
girafe^F

hyena
hyène^F

crocodile
crocodile^M

leopard
léopard^M

tiger
tigre^M

lion
lion^M

gorilla
gorille^M

tusk
défense^F

elephant
éléphant^M

trunk
trompe^F

hippopotamus
hippopotame^M

antelope
antilope^F

zebra
zèbre^M

rhinoceros
rhinocéros^M

mongoose
mangouste^F

The sea
La mer

sunscreen
écran^M solaire

sea urchin
oursin^M

starfish
étoile^F de mer^F

surfboard
planche^F de surf^M

mask
masque^M

fins
palmes^F

sunglasses
lunettes^F de soleil^M

seal
phoque^M

butterfly fish
poisson^M-papillon^M

clown fish
poisson^M-clown^M

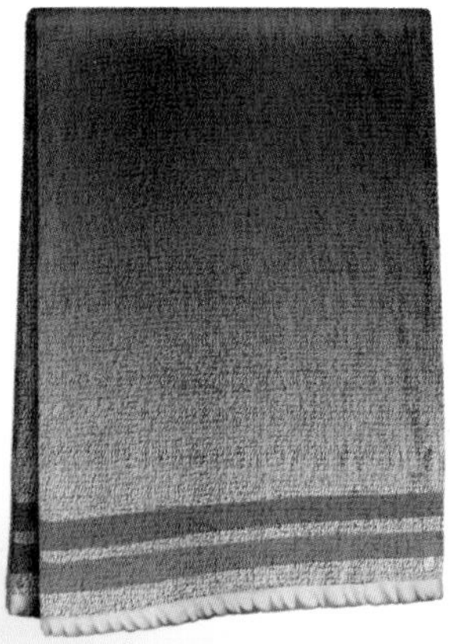

beach towel
serviette^F de plage^F

alga
algue^F

seashells
coquillages^M

shark
requin^M

shovel
pelle^F

bucket
seau^M

sand castle
château^M de sable^M

dolphin
dauphin M
skate
raie F
sea horse
hippocampe M
palm tree
palmier M
crab
crabe M
pelican
pélican M
whale
baleine F
tentacle
tentacule M
sucker
ventouse F
octopus
pieuvre F
beach umbrella
parasol M
gull
goéland M

Dinosaurs
Les dinosaures

stegosaurus
stégosaure[M]

allosaurus
allosaure[M]

pachycephalosaurus
pachycephalosaure[M]

hadrosaurus
hadrosaure[M]

deinonychus
deinonychus[M]

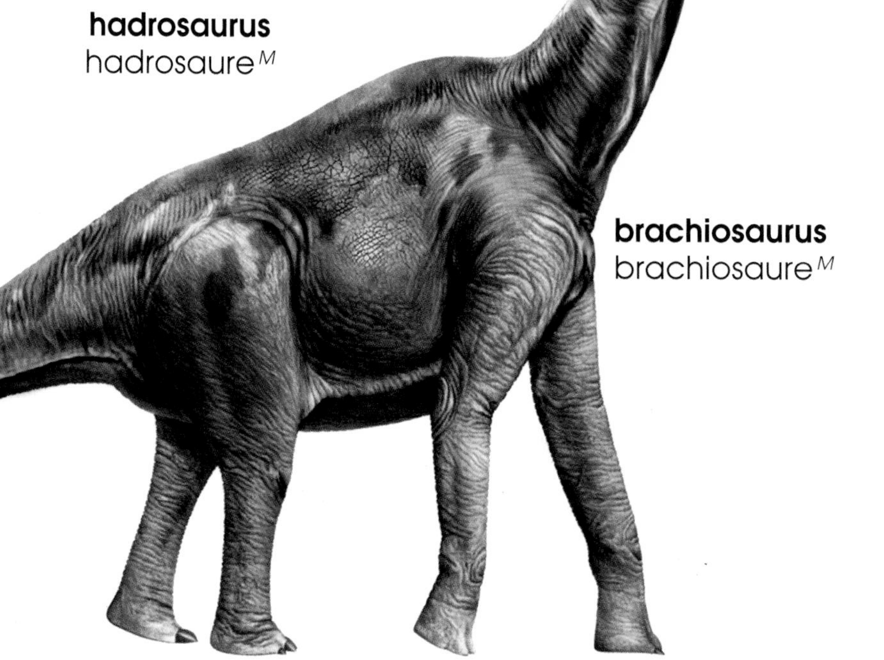

brachiosaurus
brachiosaure[M]

ankylosaurus
ankylosaure[M]

rhamphorynchus
rhamphorynchus M
spinosaurus
spinosaure M
diplodocus
diplodocus M
tyrannosaurus
tyrannosaure M
parasauroloph
parasauroloph M
triceratops
tricératops M

Plants
Les plantes

lily of the valley
muguet [M]

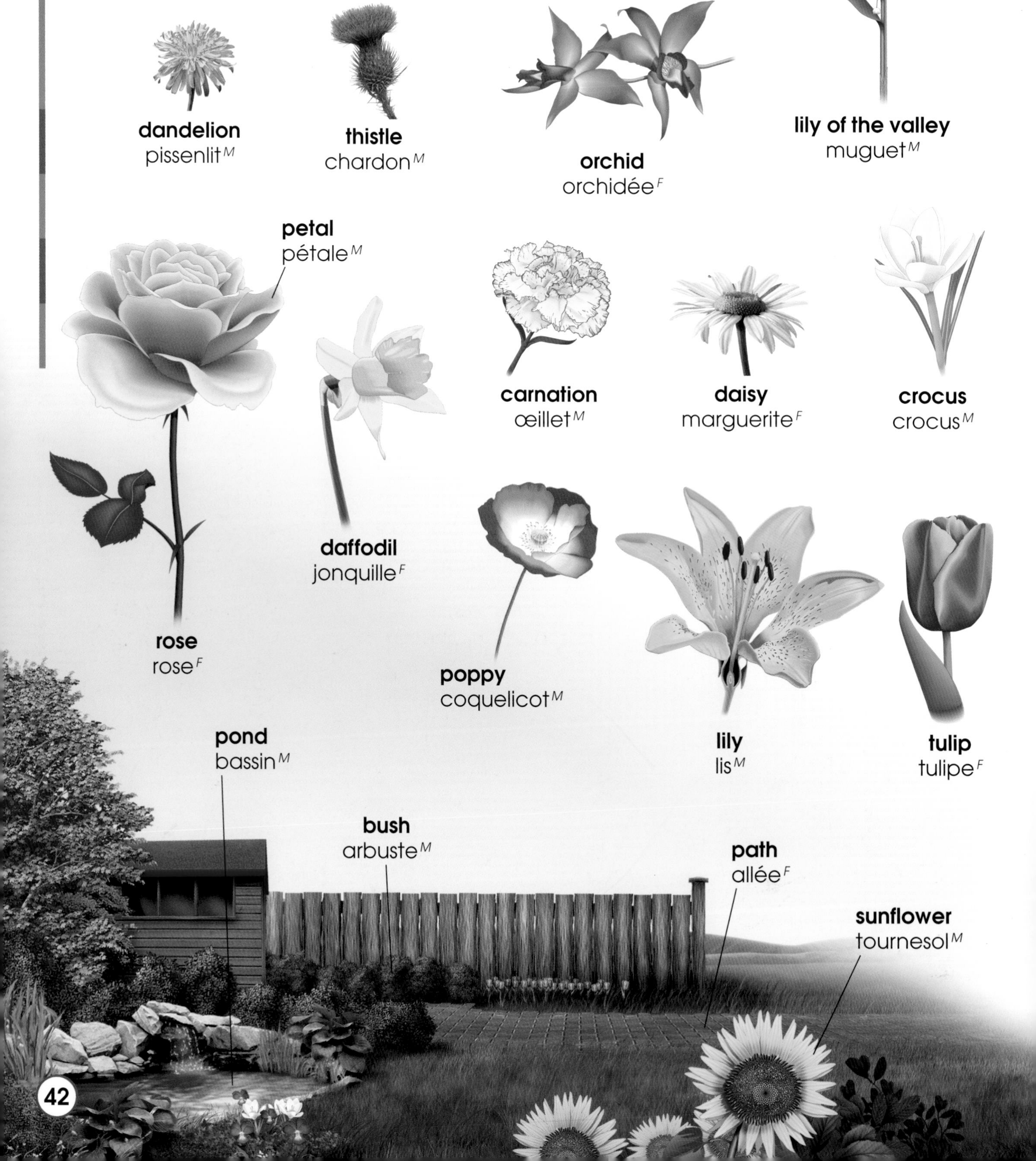
dandelion
pissenlit [M]
thistle
chardon [M]
orchid
orchidée [F]
petal
pétale [M]
carnation
œillet [M]
daisy
marguerite [F]
crocus
crocus [M]
daffodil
jonquille [F]
rose
rose [F]
poppy
coquelicot [M]
lily
lis [M]
tulip
tulipe [F]
pond
bassin [M]
bush
arbuste [M]
path
allée [F]
sunflower
tournesol [M]

watering can
arrosoir^M

bird feeder
mangeoire^F

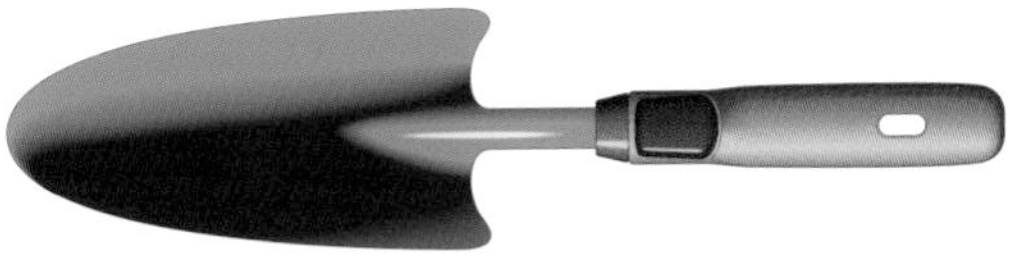

trowel
transplantoir^M

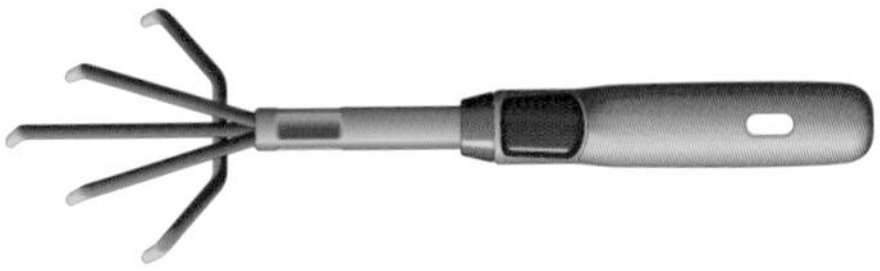

small hand cultivator
griffe^F à fleurs^F

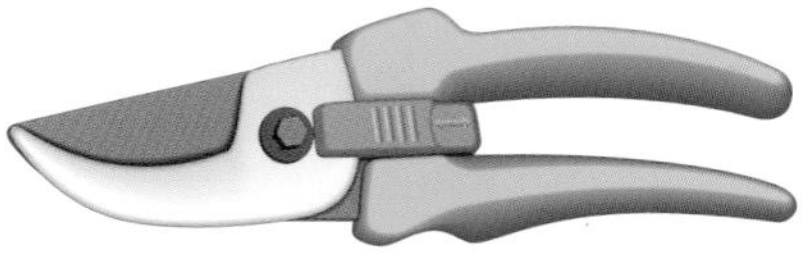

pruning shears
sécateur^M

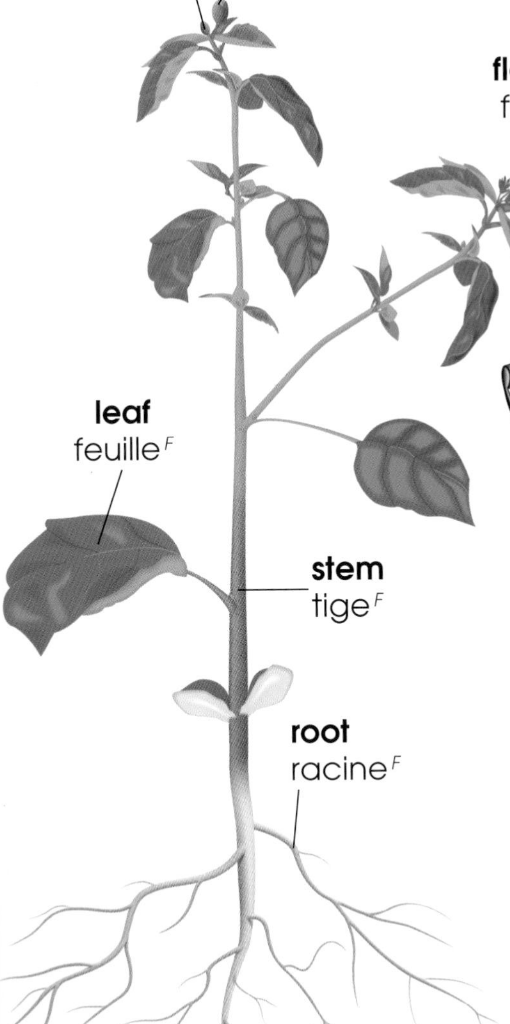

plant
plante^F

birdhouse
maison^F d'oiseau^M

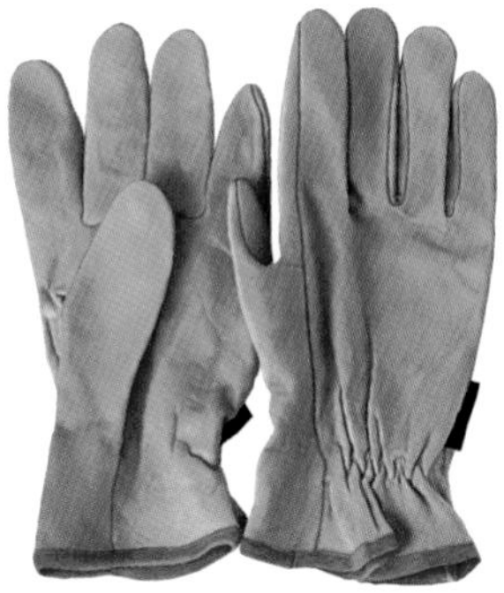

gardening gloves
gants^M de jardinage^M

spade
bêche^F

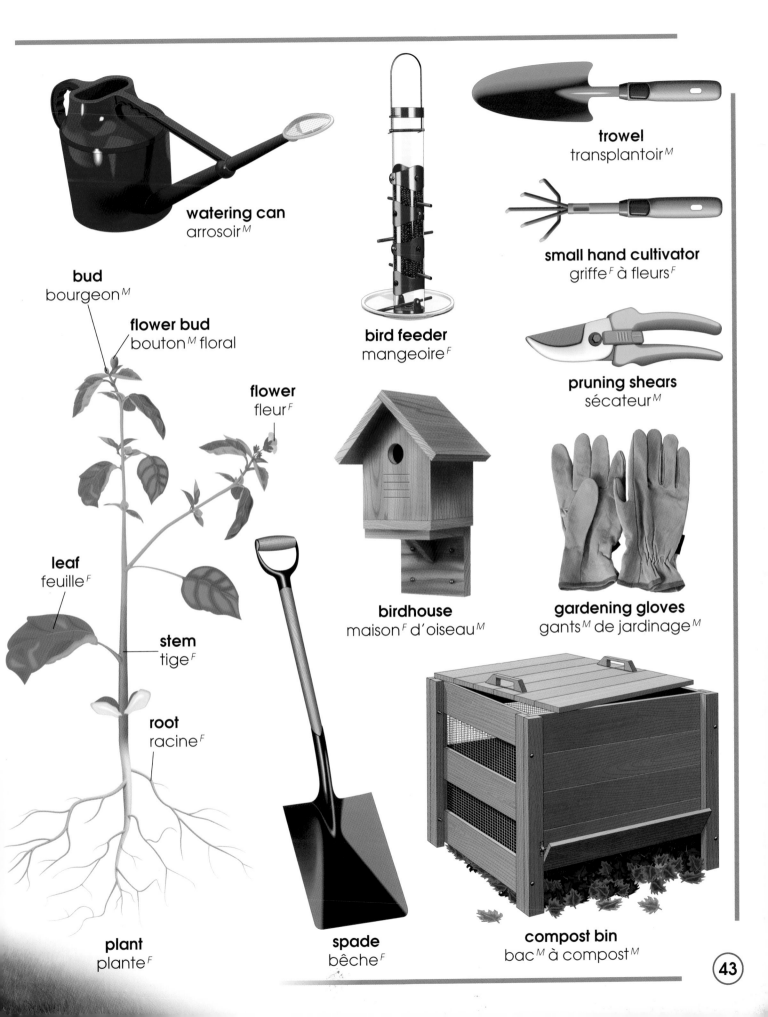

compost bin
bac^M à compost^M

Space
L'espace

planetarium
planétarium [M]

Hubble space telescope
télescope [M] spatial Hubble

Moon
Lune [F]

telescope
télescope [M]

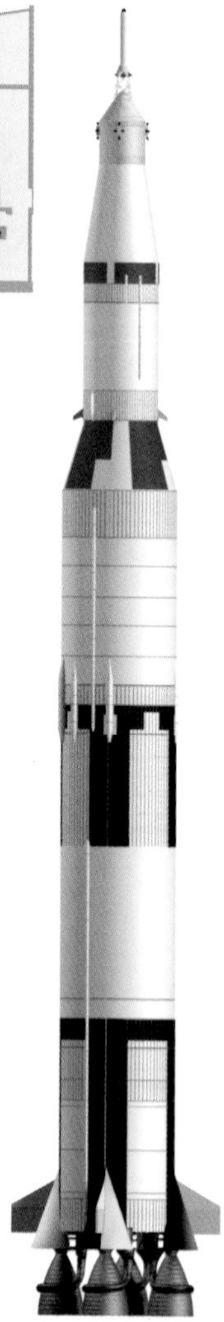

rocket
fusée [F]

new moon
nouvelle Lune [F]

crescent moon
croissant [M]

quarter moon
quartier [M]

full moon
pleine Lune [F]

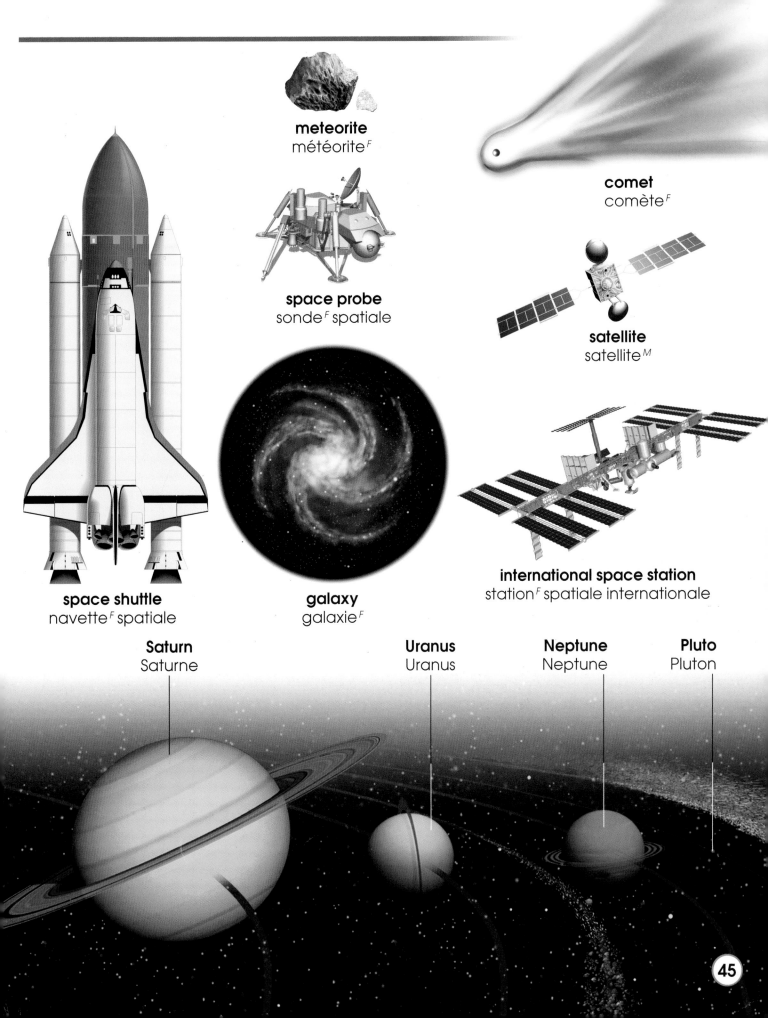

meteorite
météorite[F]

comet
comète[F]

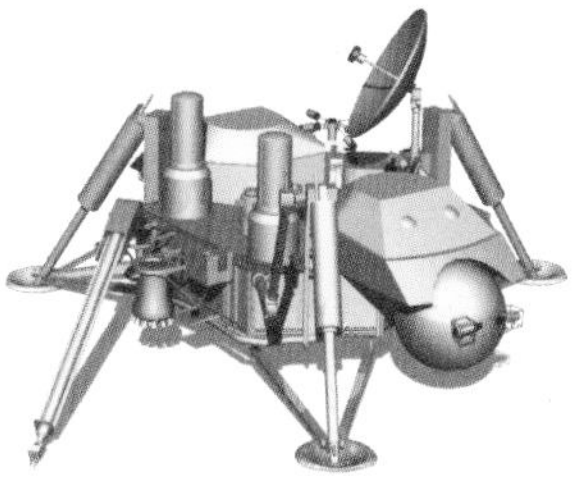

space probe
sonde[F] spatiale

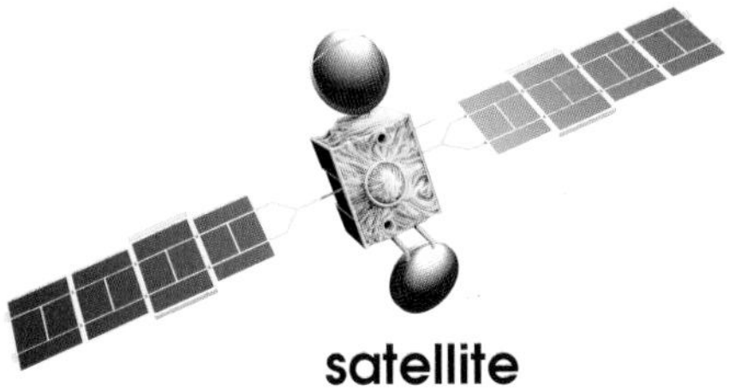

satellite
satellite[M]

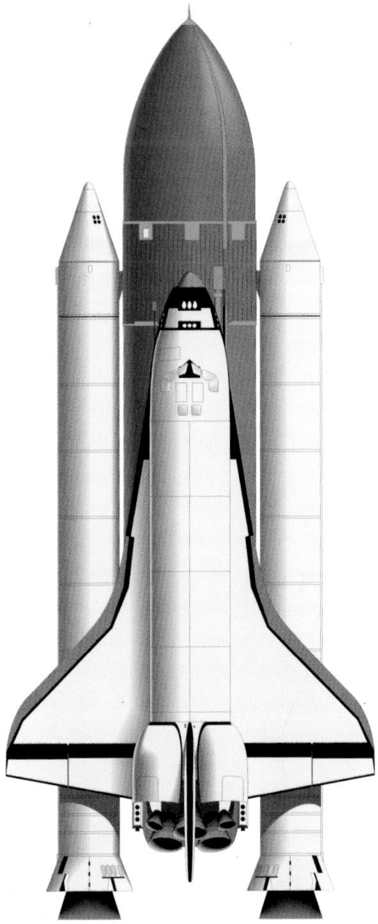

space shuttle
navette[F] spatiale

galaxy
galaxie[F]

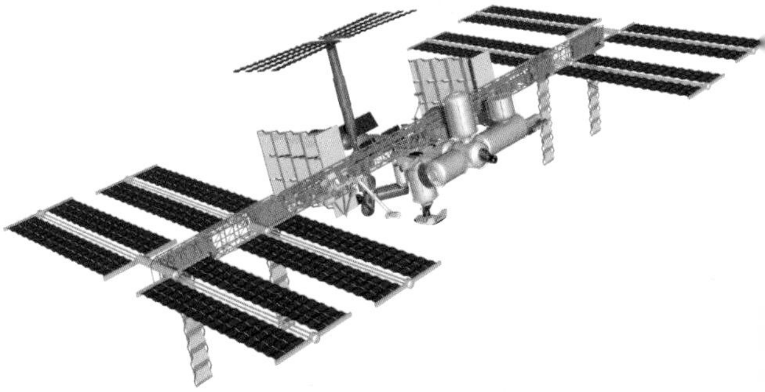

international space station
station[F] spatiale internationale

Saturn
Saturne

Uranus
Uranus

Neptune
Neptune

Pluto
Pluton

Earth's landscapes
Les paysages de la Terre

glacier
glacier^{M}

tundra
toundra^{F}

mixed forest
forêt^{F} mixte

tropical forest
forêt^{F} tropicale

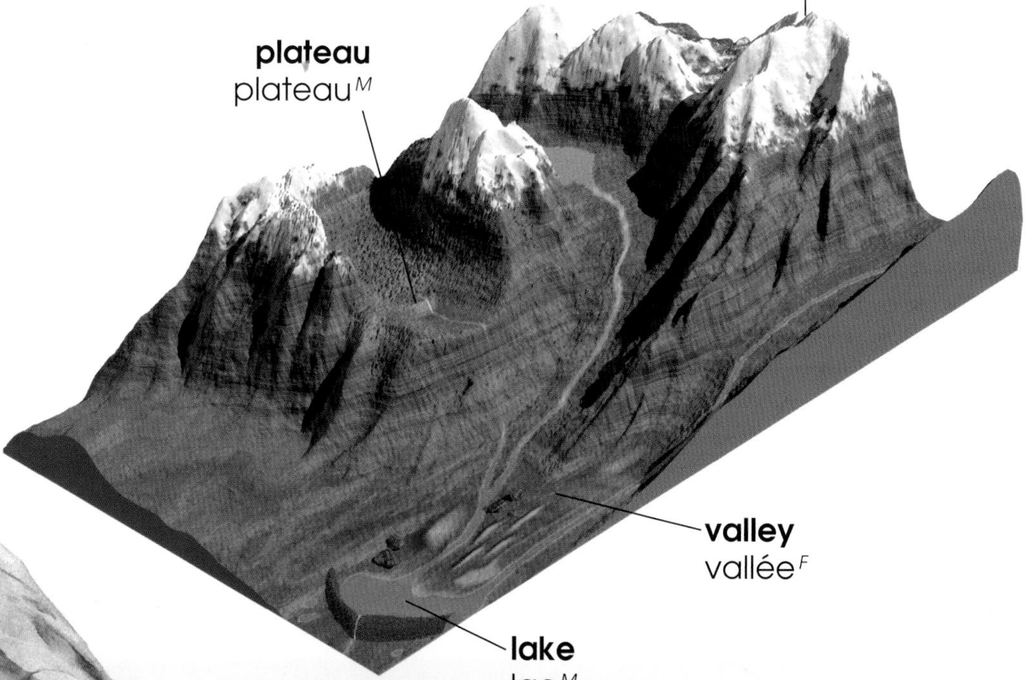

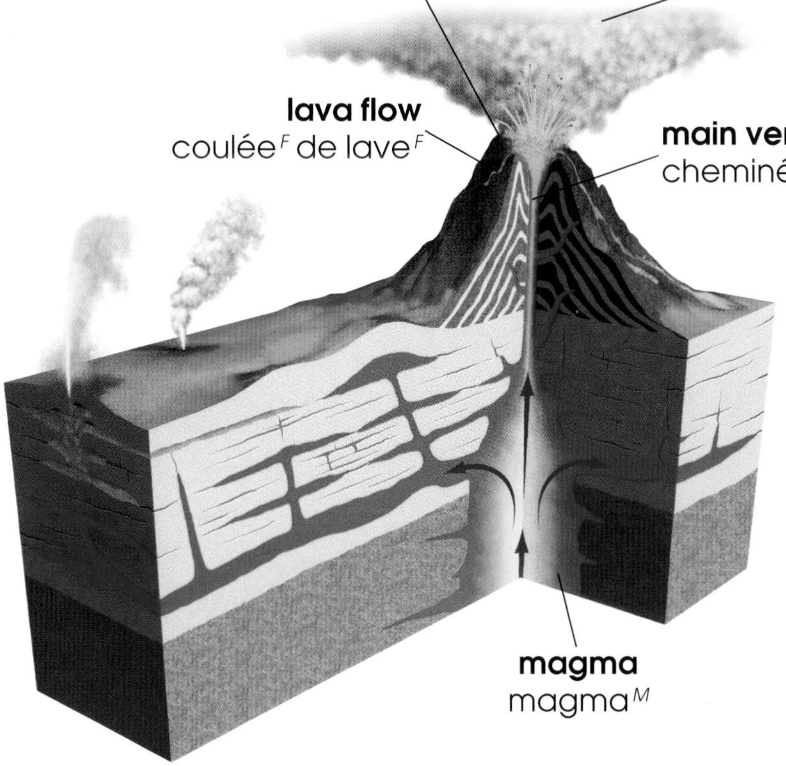

volcano
volcan^M
crater
cratère^M
cloud of volcanic ash
nuage^M de cendres^F
lava flow
coulée^F de lave^F
main vent
cheminée^F
magma
magma^M

cave
grotte^F

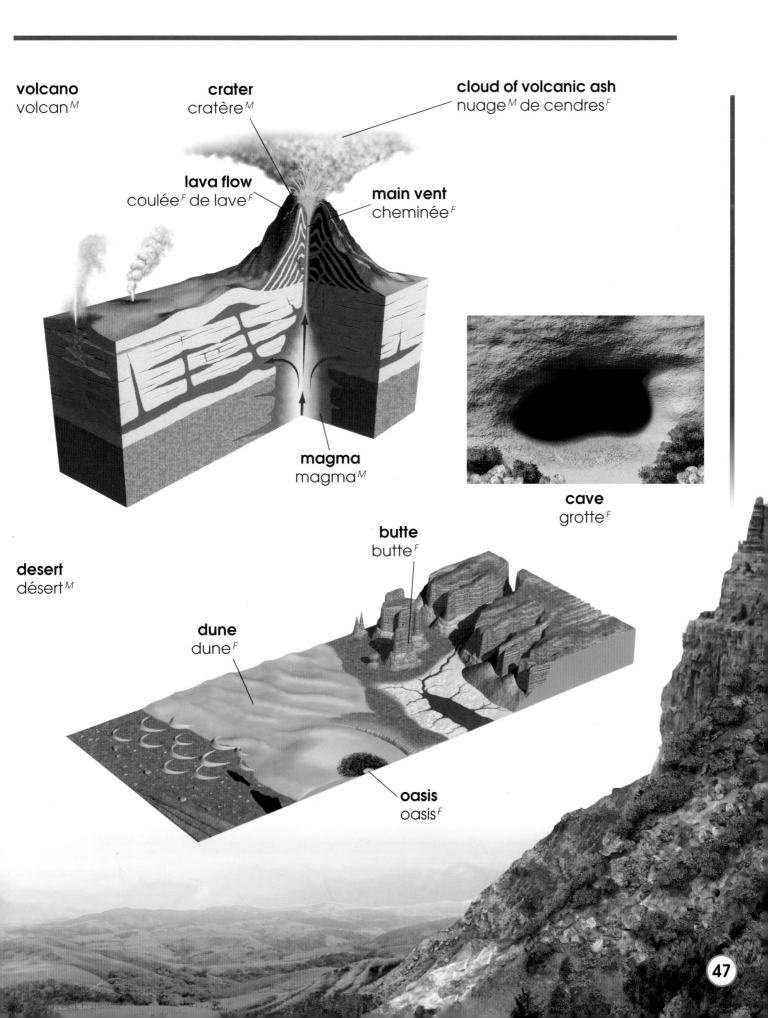

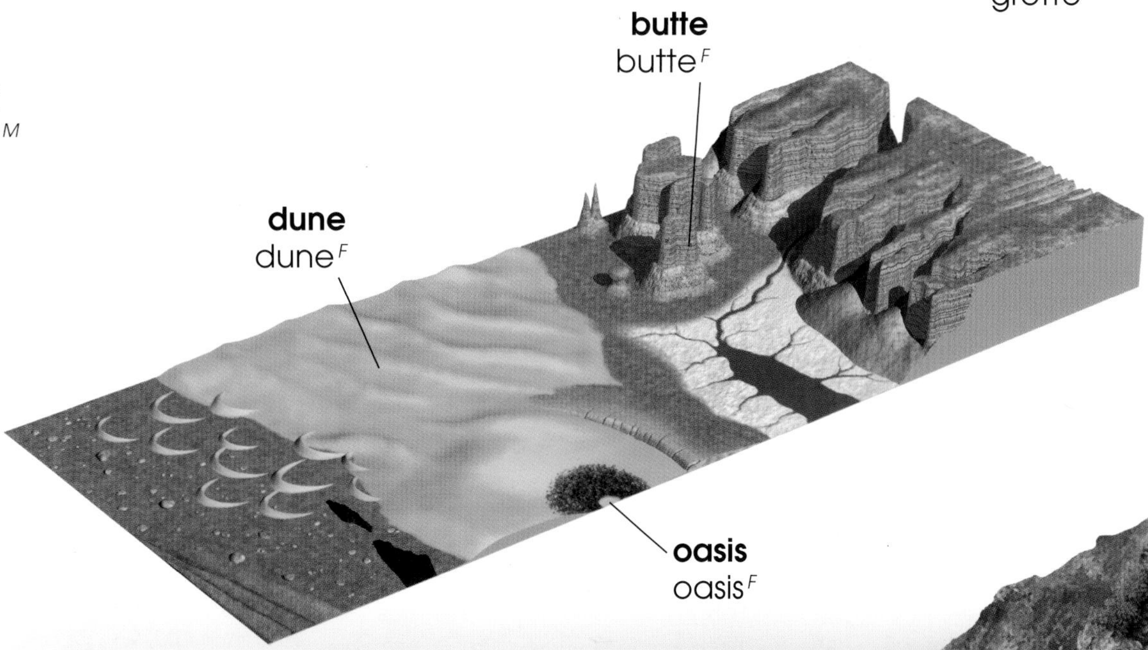

desert
désert^M
butte
butte^F
dune
dune^F
oasis
oasis^F

The weather
Le temps qu'il fait

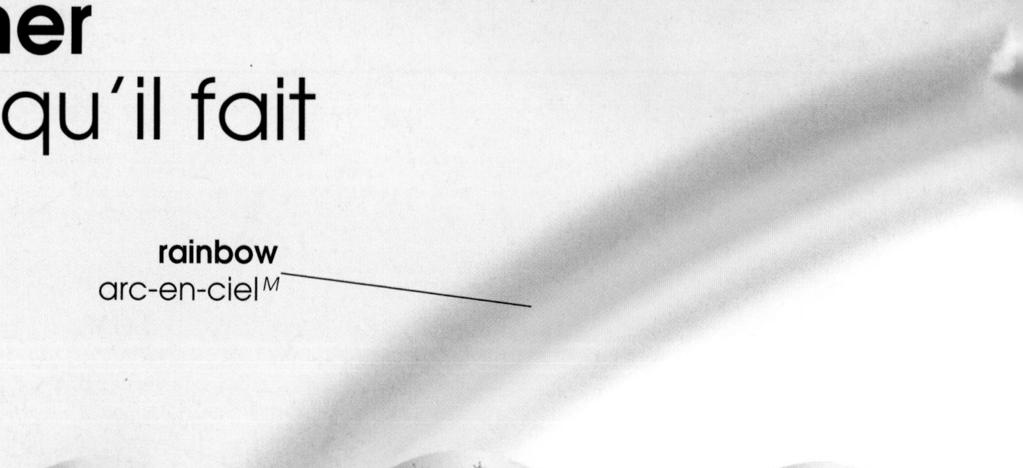

spring
printemps[M]

summer
été[M]

autumn
automne[M]

winter
hiver[M]

tropical cyclone
cyclone[M] tropical

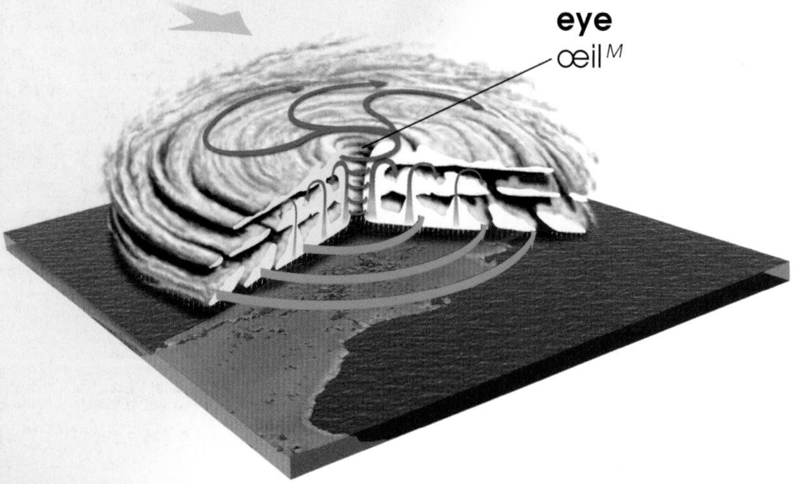

tornado
tornade[F]

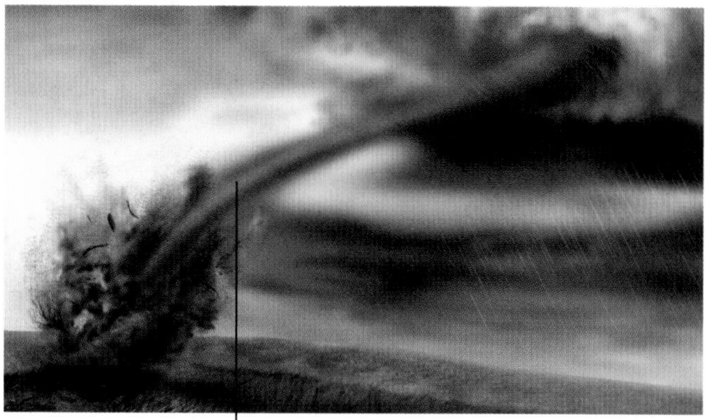

dew
rosée[F]

mist
brume[F]

fog
brouillard[M]

rime
givre[M]

drizzle
bruine[F]

rain
pluie[F]

heavy rain
pluie[F] forte

freezing rain
pluie[F] verglaçante

sleet
grésil[M]

snow
neige[F]

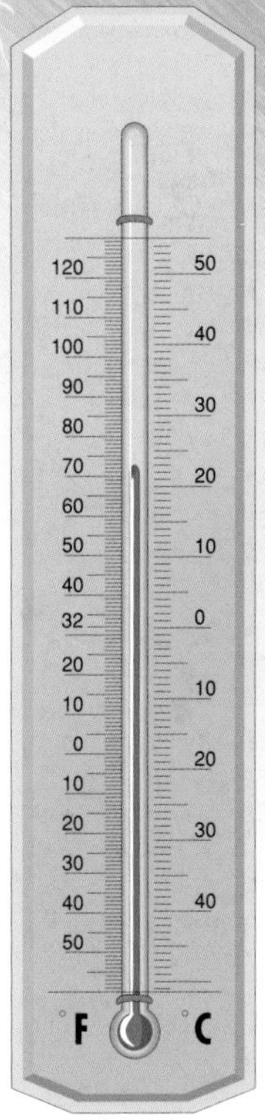

thermometer
thermomètre[M]

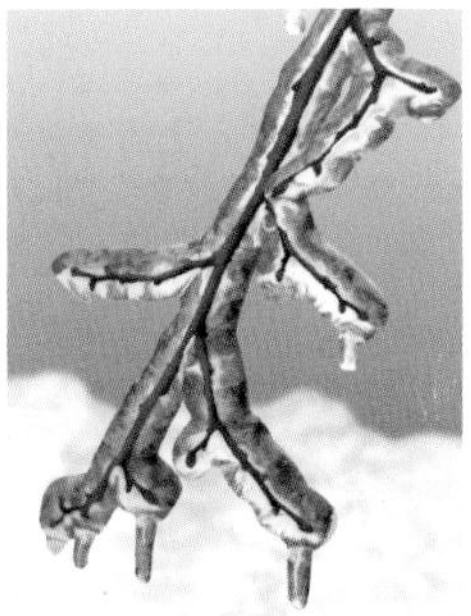

frost
verglas[M]

raindrop
goutte[F] d'eau[F]

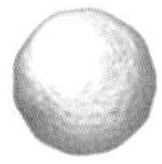

sleet
grésil[M]

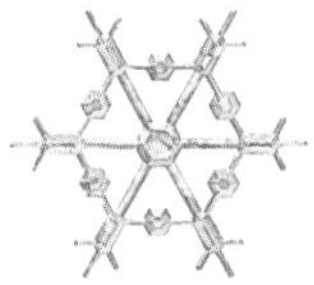

snowflake
flocon[M] de neige[F]

hail
grêlon[M]

Transportation on water
Les transports sur l'eau

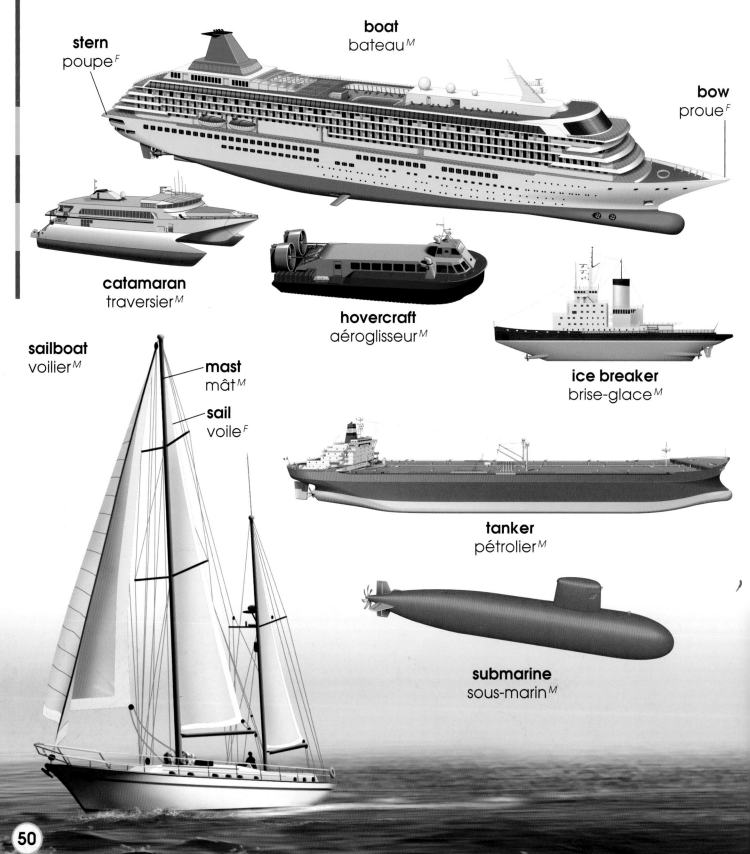

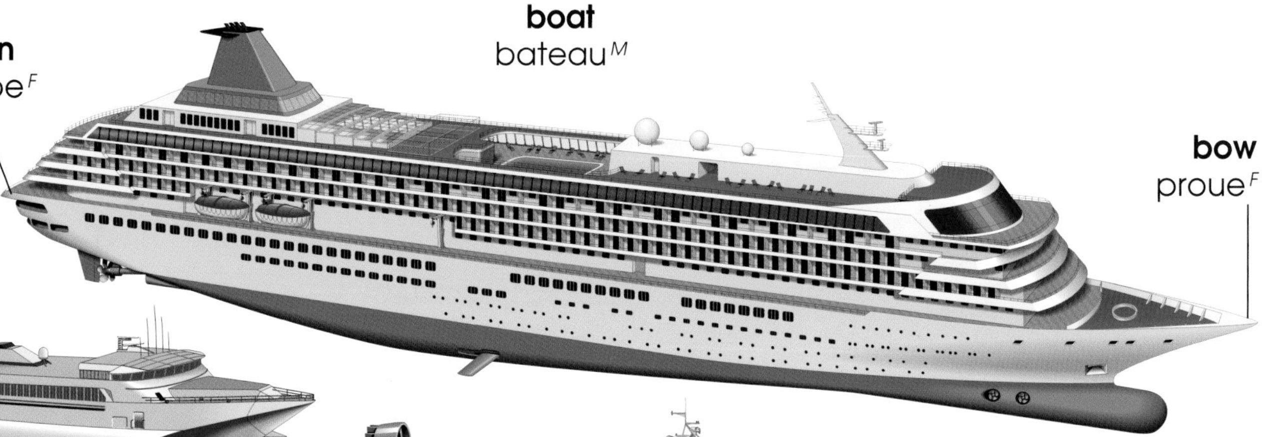

boat
bateau^M

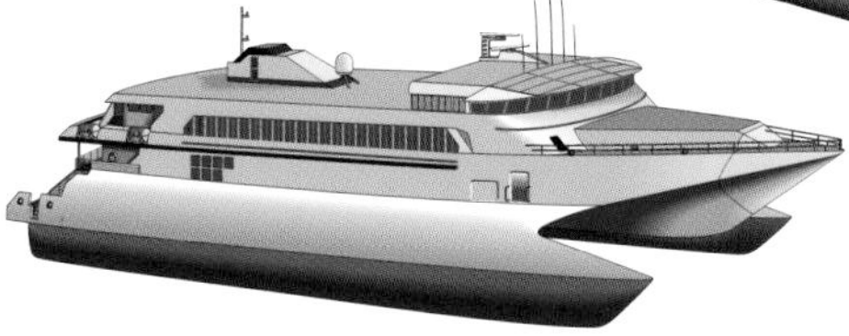

catamaran
traversier^M

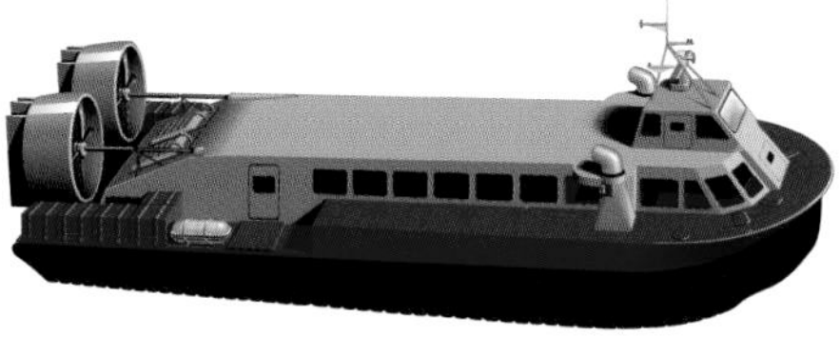

hovercraft
aéroglisseur^M

ice breaker
brise-glace^M

sailboat
voilier^M

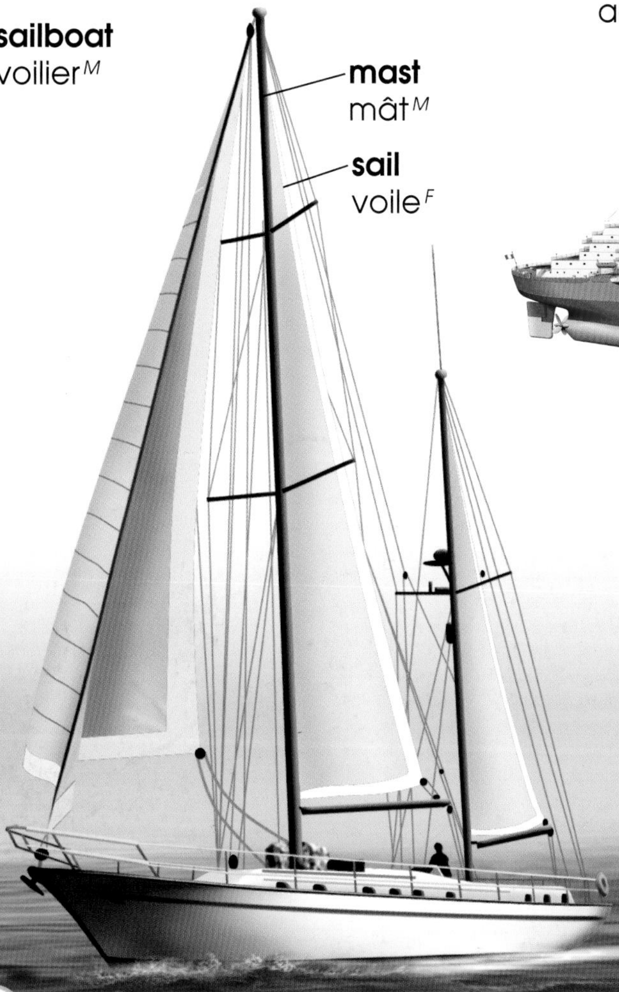

tanker
pétrolier^M

submarine
sous-marin^M

anchor
ancre^{F}

life buoy
bouée^{F} de sauvetage^{M}

personal flotation device
gilet^{M} de sauvetage^{M}

personal watercraft
motomarine^{F}

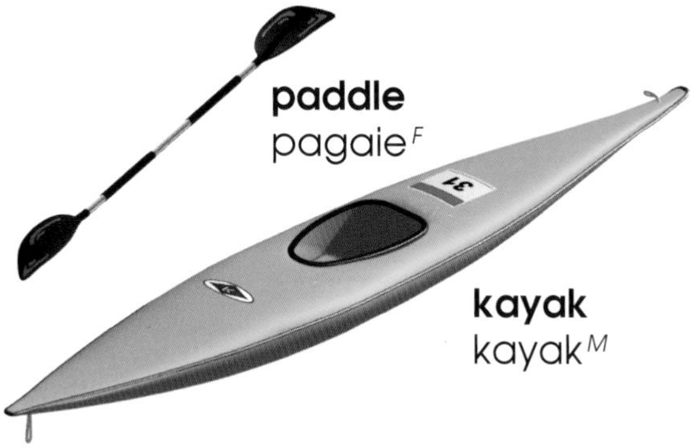

paddle
pagaie^{F}

kayak
kayak^{M}

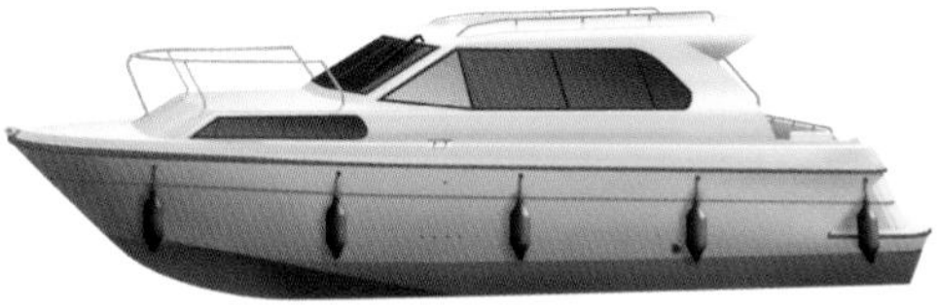

yacht
yacht^{M}

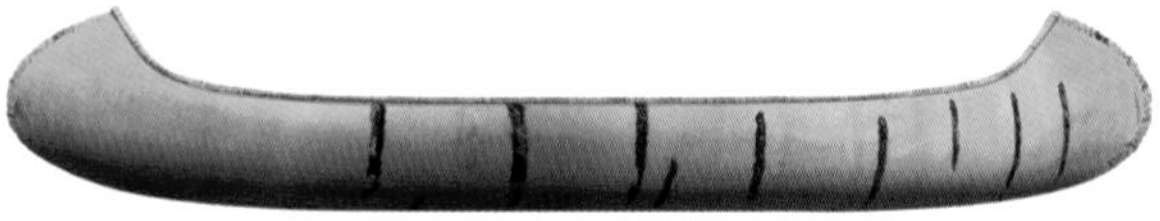

canoe
canot^{M}

lighthouse
phare^{M}

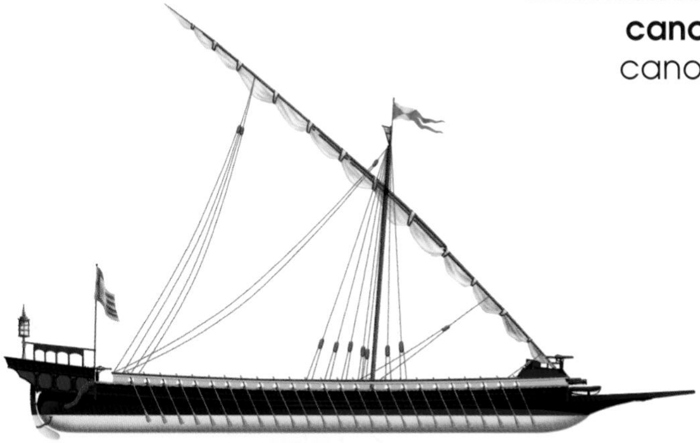

galley
galère^{F}

caravel
caravelle^{F}

container ship
navire^{M} porte-conteneurs^{M}

speedboat
hors-bord^{M}

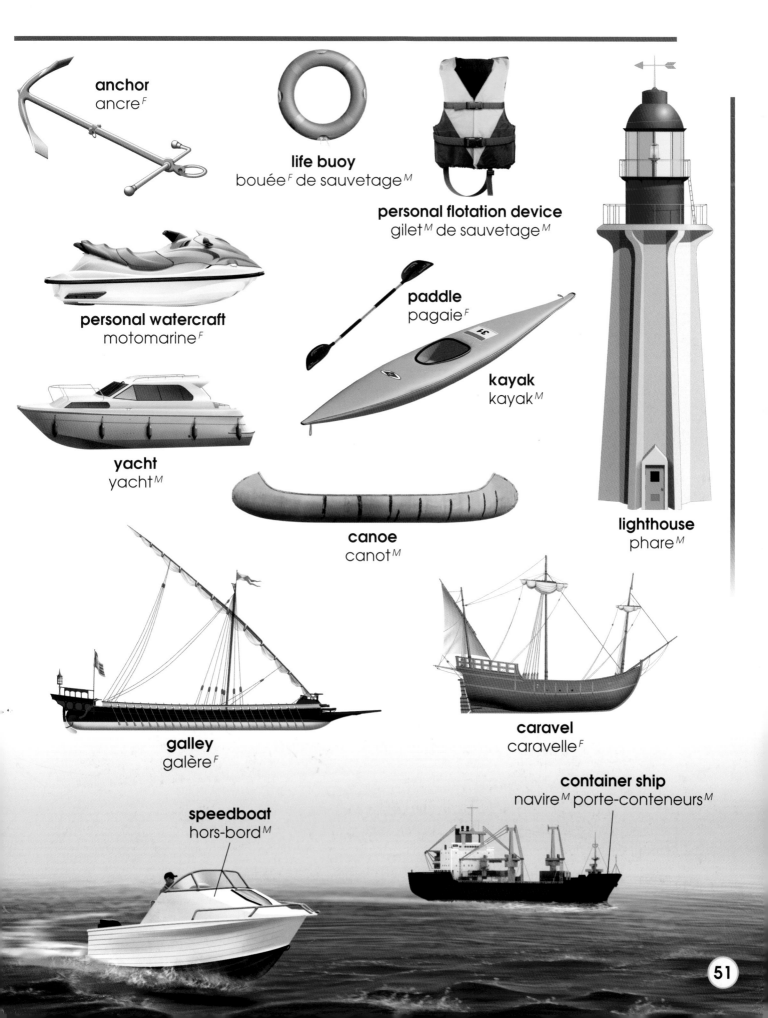

Transportation in the air
Les transports dans les airs

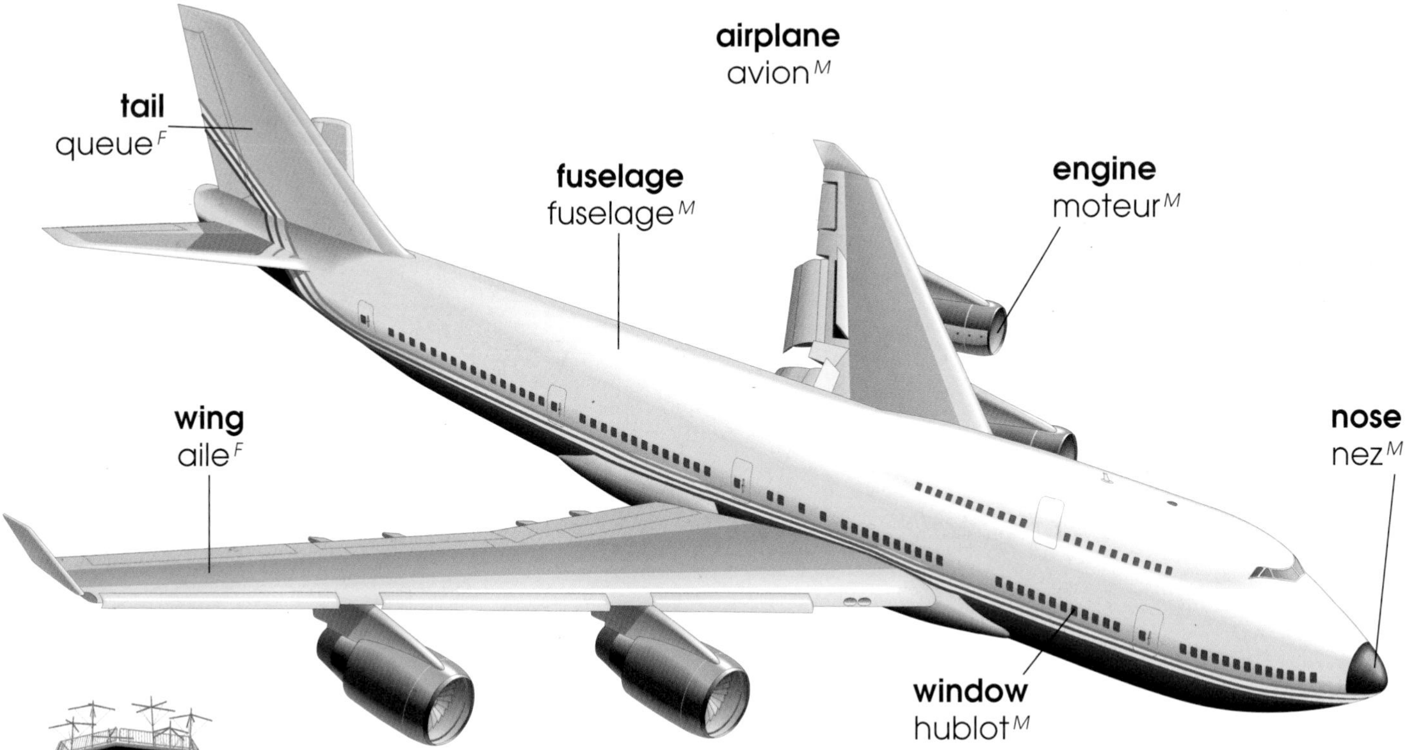

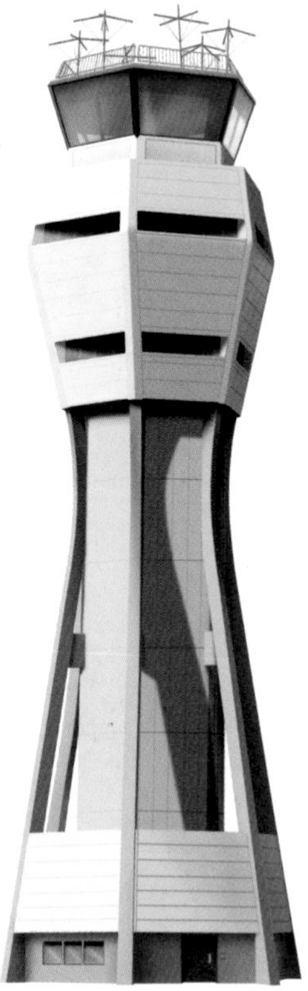

control tower
tour^{F} de contrôle^{M}

passenger transfer vehicle
transbordeur^{M}

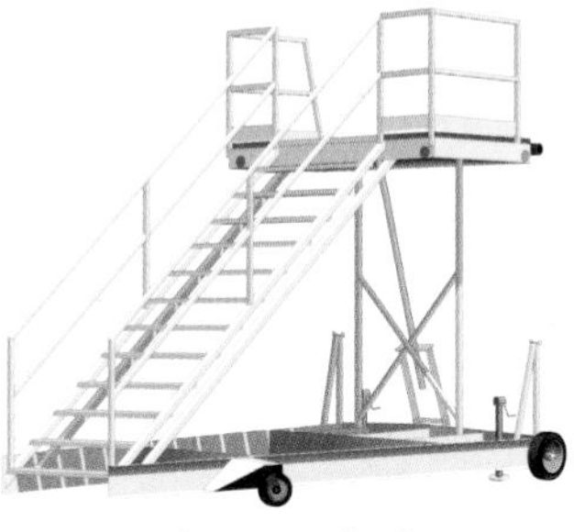

universal step
escalier^{M} d'accès^{M}

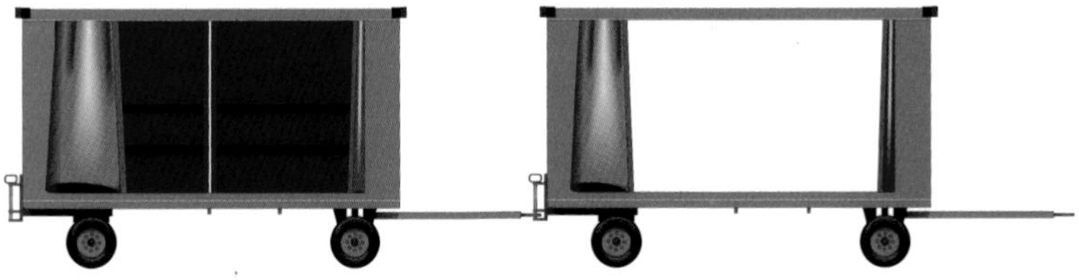

baggage trailer
chariot^{M} à bagages^{M}

tow tractor
tracteur^{M}

seaplane
hydravion^{M}

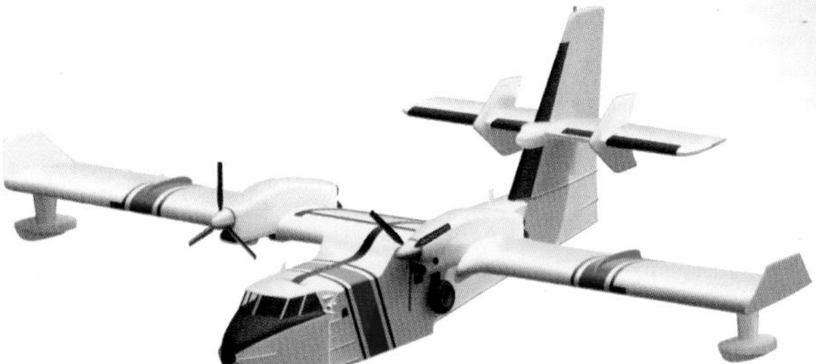

fire-fighting aircraft
avion^{M}-citerne^{F}

business aircraft
avion^{M} d'affaires^{F}

cargo aircraft
avion^{M}-cargo^{M}

hot-air balloon
montgolfière^{F}

biplane
biplan^{M}

light aircraft
avion^{M} léger

helicopter
hélicoptère^{M}

Transportation on land
Les transports sur la terre

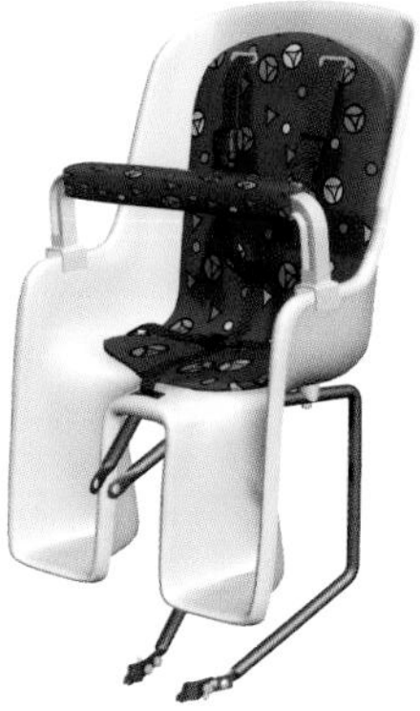

child carrier
siège^{M} de vélo^{M} pour enfant^{M}

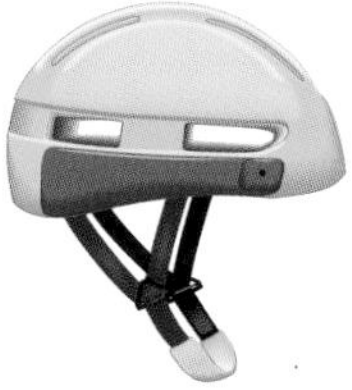

bicycle helmet
casque^{M} de vélo^{M}

bicycle
bicyclette^{F}

brake
frein^{M}

pedal
pédale^{F}

handlebars
guidon^{M}

seat
selle^{F}

drive chain
chaîne^{F}

motorcycle helmet
casque^{M} de moto^{F}

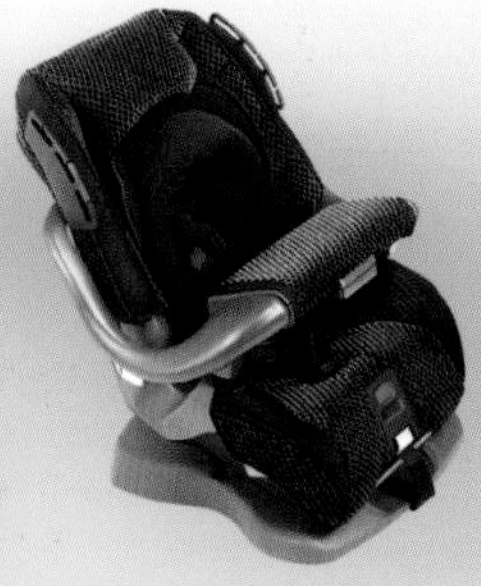

child safety seat
siège^{M} de sécurité^{F} pour enfant^{M}

motorcycle
moto^{F}

motor scooter
scooter^{M}

highway crossing
passage^{M} à niveau^{M}

railroad track
voie^{F} ferrée

subway train
rame^{F} de métro^{M}

school bus
autobus^{M} scolaire

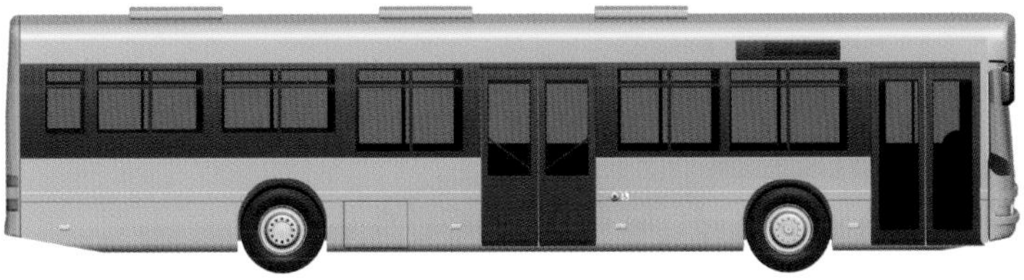

city bus
autobus^{M}

streetcar
tramway^{M}

train
train^{M}

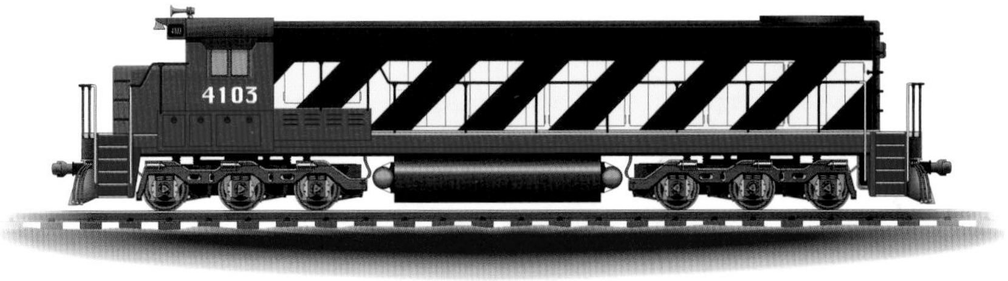

locomotive
locomotive^{F}

minivan
fourgonnette^{F}

pickup truck
camionnette^{F}

car
voiture^{F}

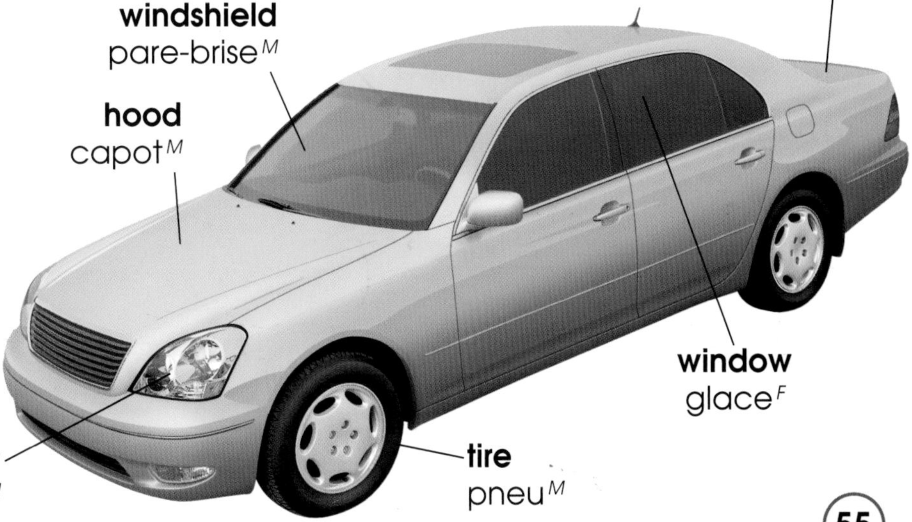

The city
La ville

one-storey house
maison[F] de plain-pied[M]

condominiums
appartements[M] en copropriété[F]

semidetached house
maison[F] jumelée

bell tower
clocher[M]

church
église[F]

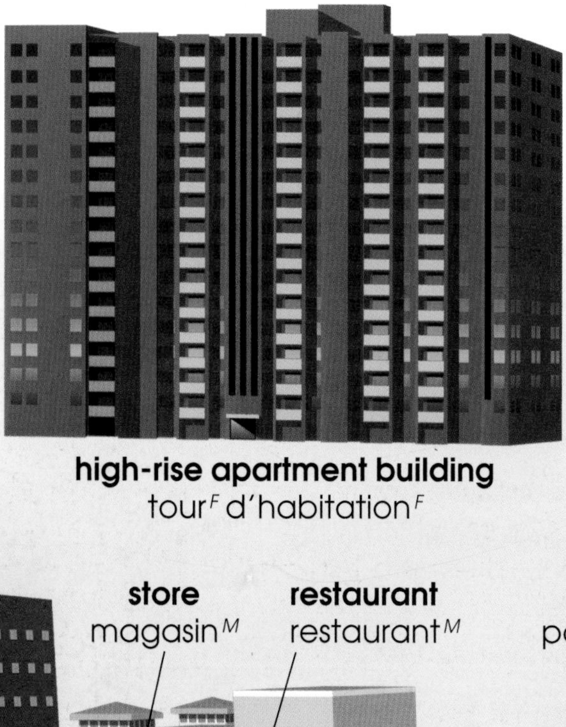

high-rise apartment building
tour[F] d'habitation[F]

hotel
hôtel[M]

fire station
caserne[F] de pompiers[M]

store
magasin[M]

restaurant
restaurant[M]

police station
poste[M] de police[F]

roadwork
travaux^{M}

pedestrian crossing
passage^{M} pour piétons^{M}

factory
usine^{F}

stop
arrêt^{M}

school zone
zone^{F} scolaire

fire hydrant
borne^{F} d'incendie^{M}

traffic lights
feu^{M} de circulation^{F}

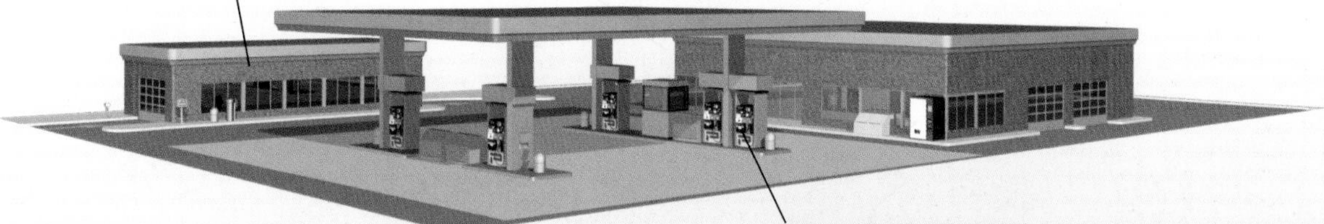

car wash
lave-auto^{M}

service station
station^{F}-service^{M}

gasoline pump
distributeur^{M} d'essence^{F}

skyscraper
gratte-ciel^{M}

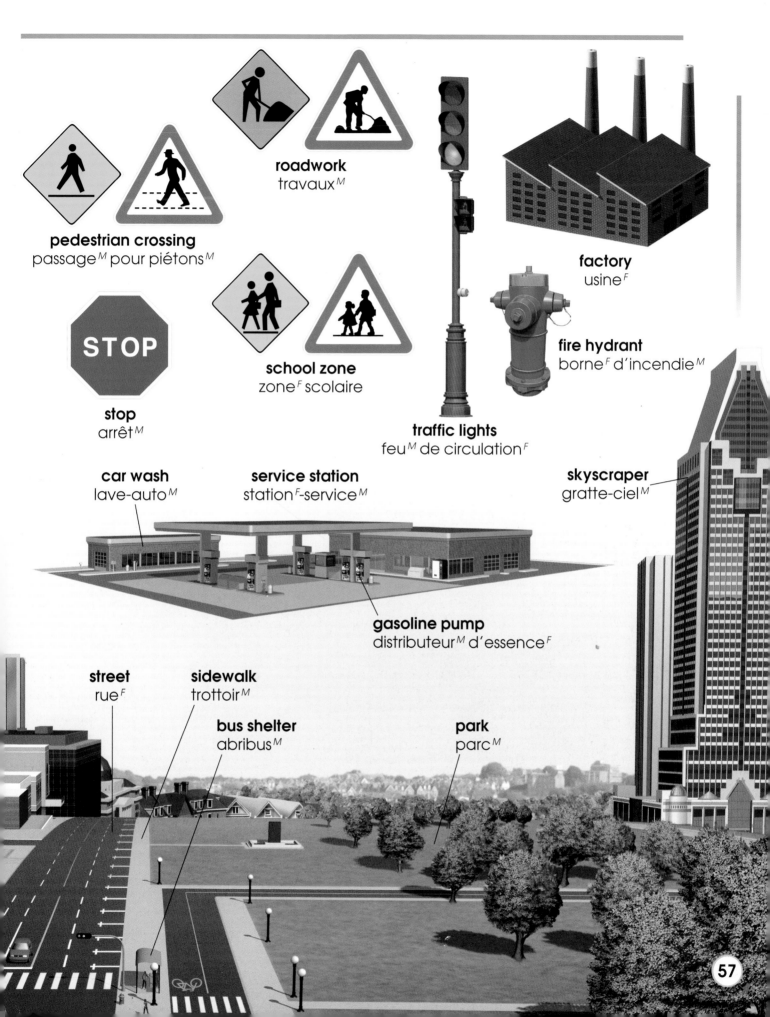

street
rue^{F}

sidewalk
trottoir^{M}

bus shelter
abribus^{M}

park
parc^{M}

Trades
Les métiers

driver
pilote[M]

backhoe loader
pelle[F] mécanique

hard hat
casque[M] de sécurité[F]

road worker
ouvrier[M] de voirie[F]

racing car
voiture[F] de course[F]

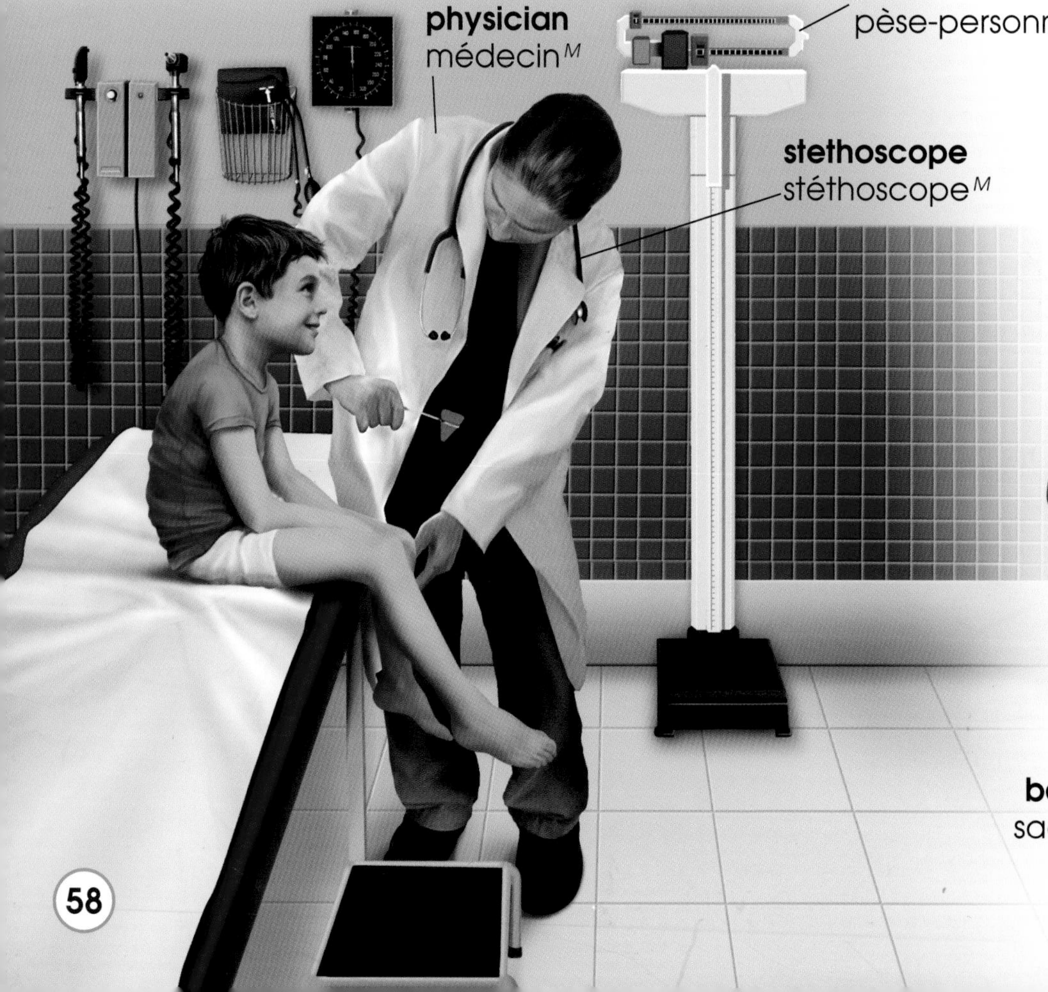

physician
médecin[M]

scale
pèse-personne[M]

stethoscope
stéthoscope[M]

mail carrier
factrice[F]

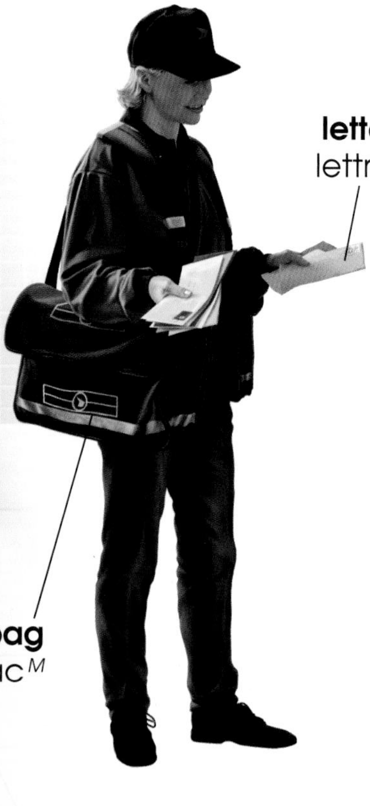

letter
lettre[F]

bag
sac[M]

firefighter
pompier^{M}

helmet
casque^{M}

mask
masque^{M}

compressed-air cylinder
bouteille^{F} d'air^{M} comprimé

hatchet
hache^{F}

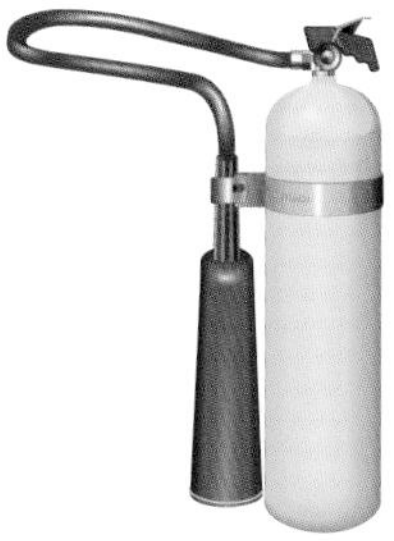

fire extinguisher
extincteur^{M}

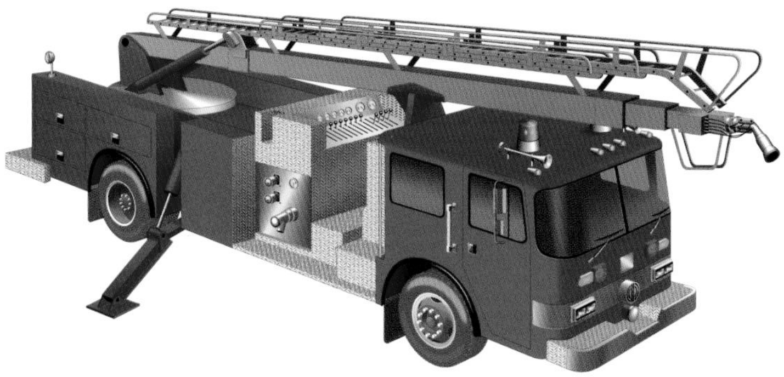

fire truck
camion^{M} d'incendie^{M}

fire hose
tuyau^{M} d'incendie^{M}

duty belt
ceinturon^{M} de service^{M}

police car
voiture^{F} de police^{F}

police officer
agent^{M} de police^{F}

astronaut
astronaute^{M}

School
L'école

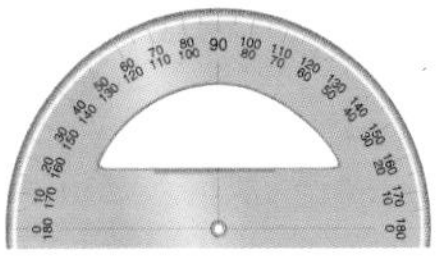

protractor
rapporteur^{M} d'angle^{M}

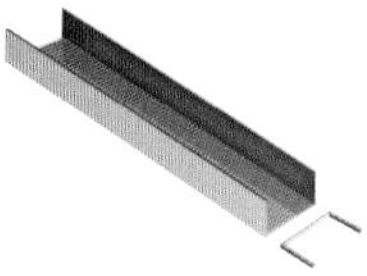

staples
agrafes^{F}

stapler
agrafeuse^{F}

calculator
calculatrice^{F}

clip
pince-notes^{M}

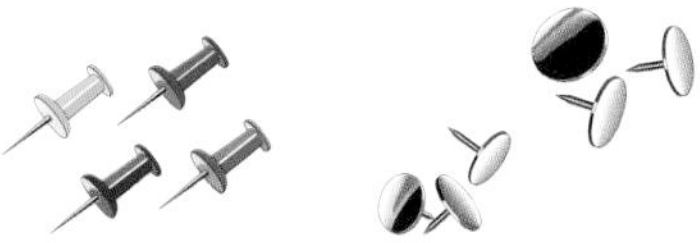

thumb tacks
punaises^{F}

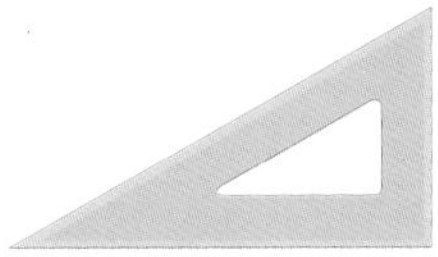

framing square
équerre^{F}

paper punch
perforatrice^{F}

bulletin board
babillard^{M}

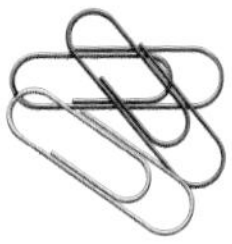

paper clips
trombones^{M}

chalk
craie^{F}

globe
globe^{M} terrestre

blackboard eraser
brosse^{F}

backpack
sac^{M} à dos^{M}

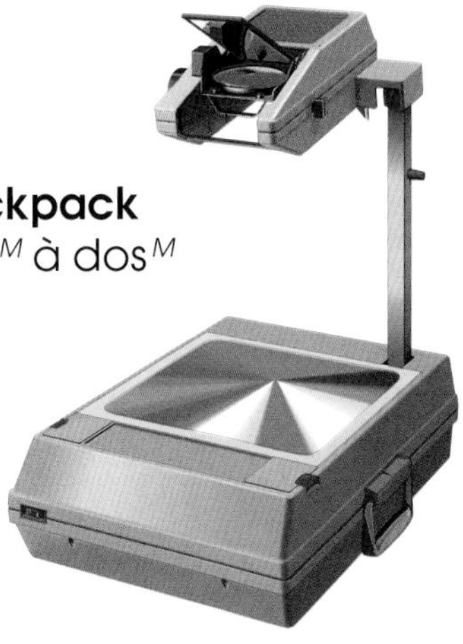

overhead projector
rétroprojecteur^{M}

clock
pendule^{F}

chalk board
tableau^{M}

geographical map
carte^{F} géographique

student
élève^{M}

chair
chaise^{F}

student's desk
bureau^{M} d'élève^{M}

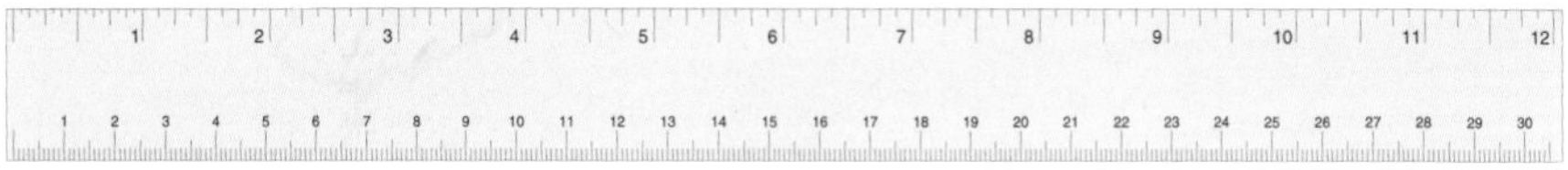

ruler
règle^{F}

pencil
crayon^{M}

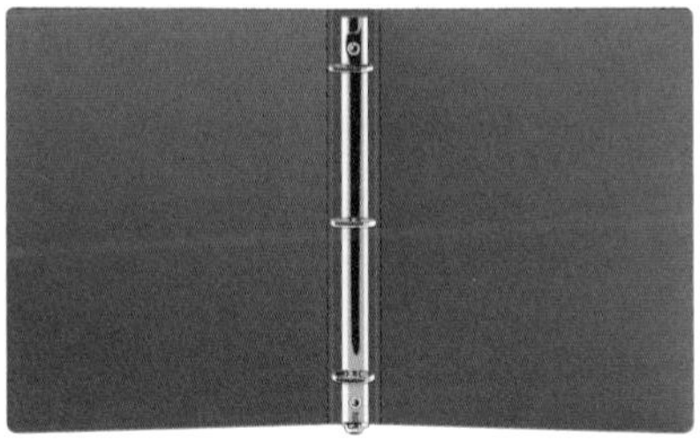

ring binder
reliure^{F} à anneaux^{M}

pencil sharpener
taille-crayon^{M}

eraser
gomme^{F}

mechanical pencil
porte-mine^{M}

ballpoint pen
stylo^{M}-bille^{F}

fountain pen
stylo^{M}-plume^{F}

loose-leaf paper
feuilles^{F} mobiles

notebook
cahier^{M}

spiral notebook
reliure^{F} spirale^{F}

marker
marqueur^{M}

highlighter pen
surligneur^{M}

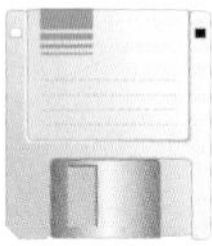

diskette
disquette^{F}

eraser holder
porte-gomme^{M}

computer
ordinateur^{M}

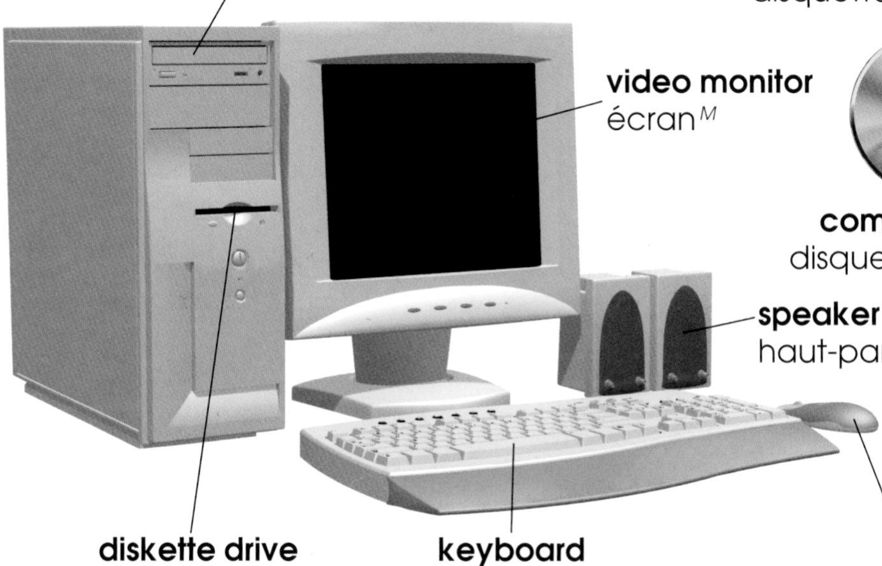

CD/DVD drive
lecteur^{M} de CD/DVD^{M}

video monitor
écran^{M}

speaker
haut-parleur^{M}

diskette drive
lecteur^{M} de disquette^{F}

keyboard
clavier^{M}

mouse
souris^{F}

compact disc
disque^{M} compact

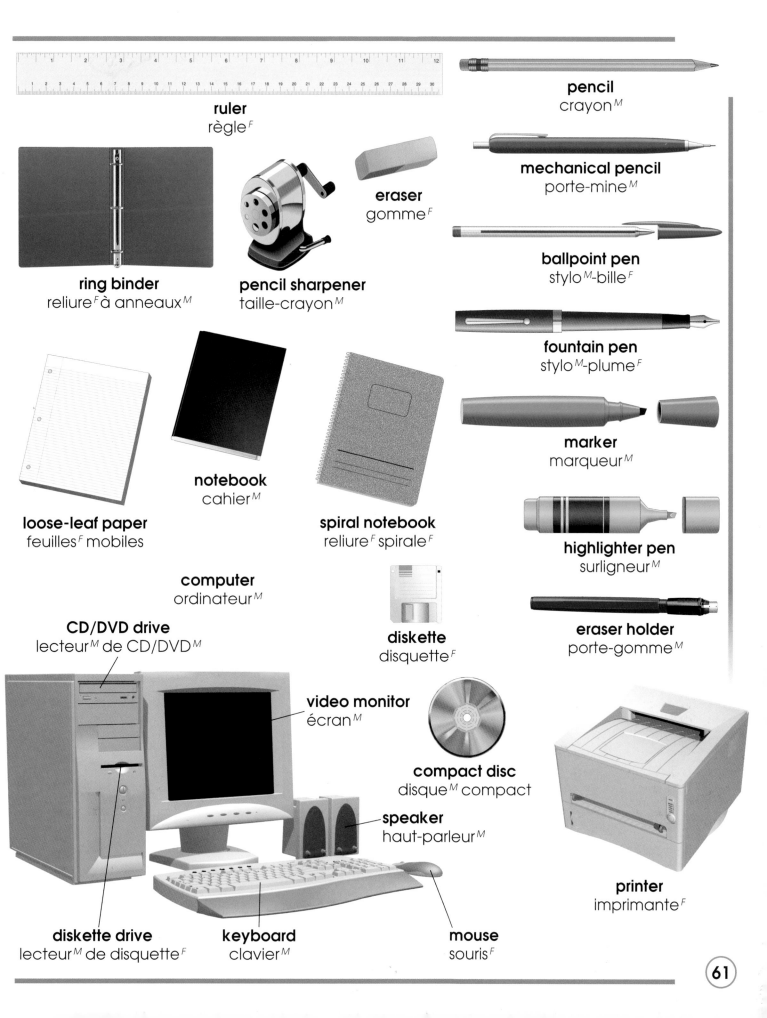

printer
imprimante^{F}

Colors and shapes
Les couleurs et les formes

yellow
jaune[M]

green
vert[M]

orange
orange[M]

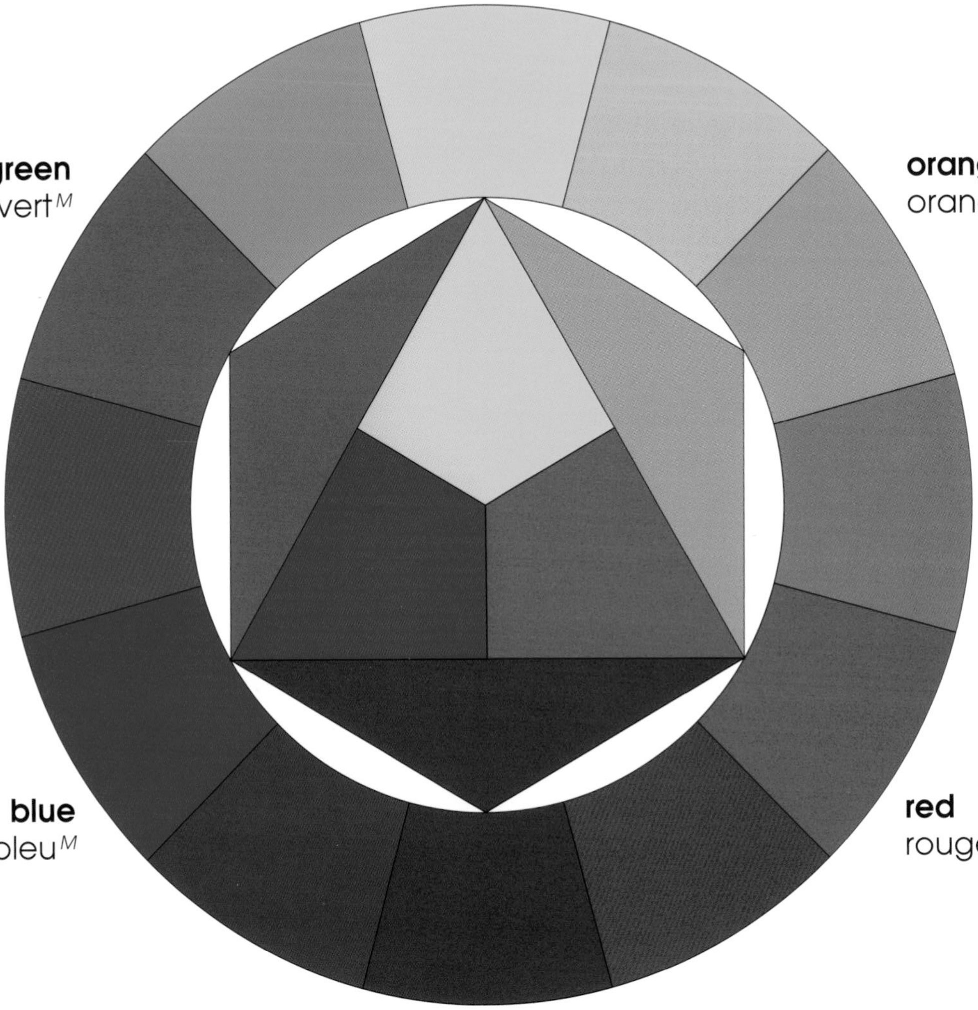

blue
bleu[M]

red
rouge[M]

purple
violet[M]

white + black = gray
blanc[M] + noir[M] = gris[M]

yellow + blue = green
jaune[M] + bleu[M] = vert[M]

yellow + red = orange
jaune[M] + rouge[M] = orange[M]

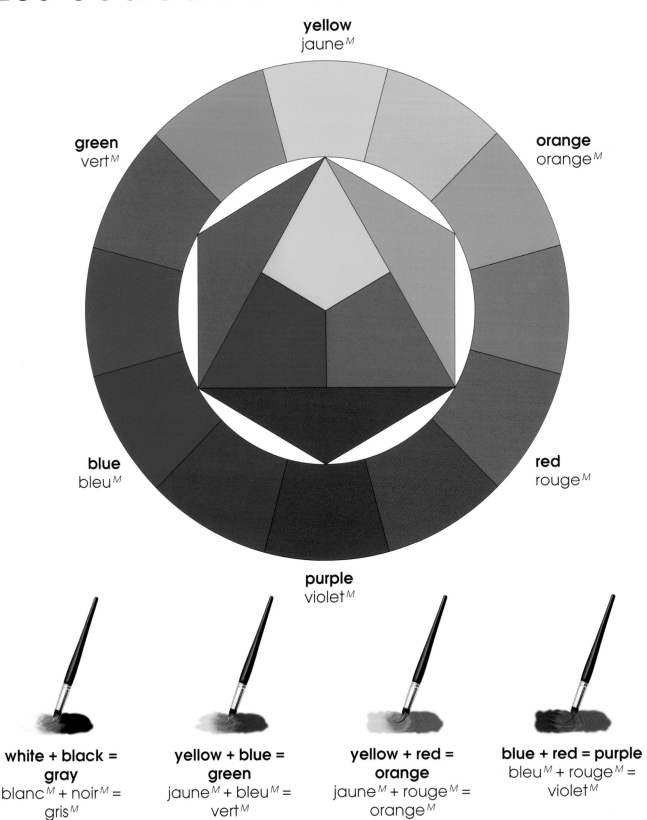

blue + red = purple
bleu[M] + rouge[M] = violet[M]

circle
cercle^M

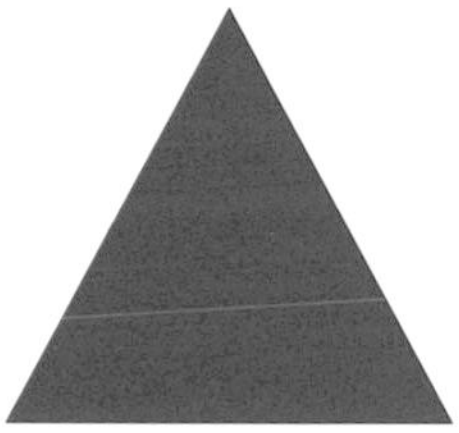

triangle
triangle^M

square
carré^M

rectangle
rectangle^M

rhombus
losange^M

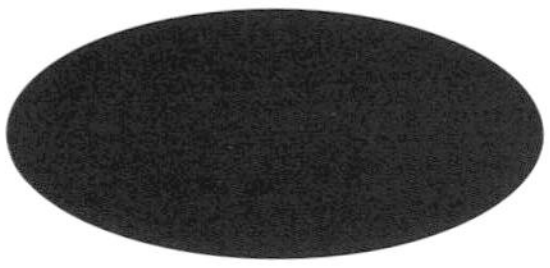

oval
ovale^M

trapezoid
trapèze^M

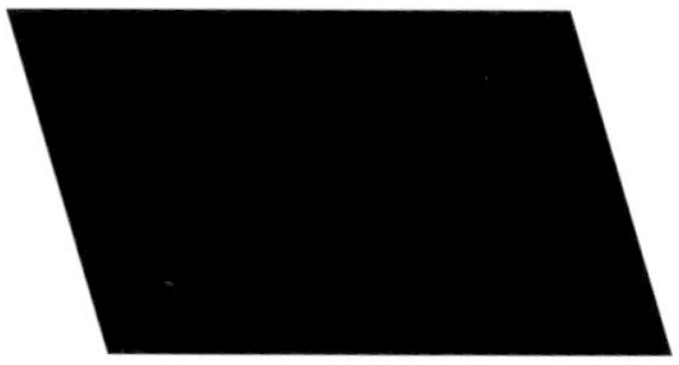

parallelogram
parallélogramme^M

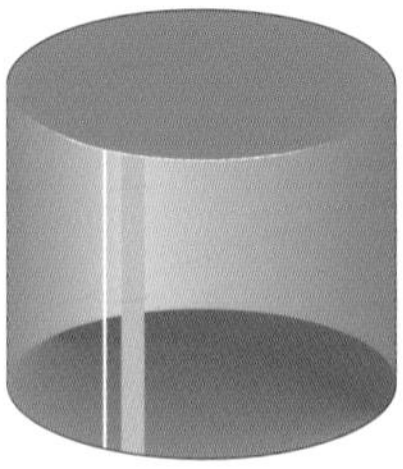

cylinder
cylindre^M

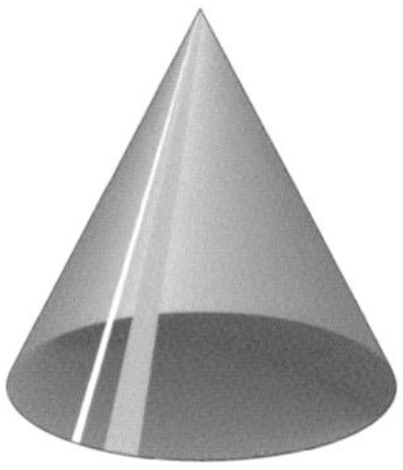

cone
cône^M

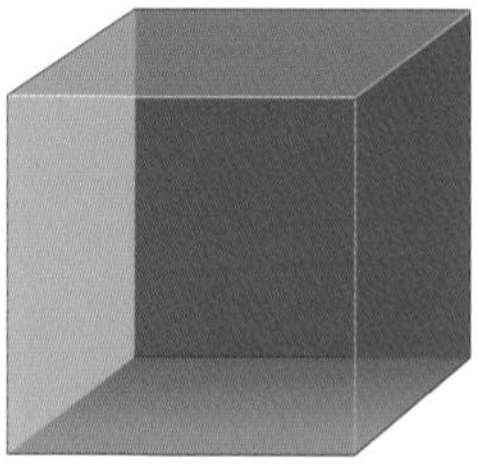

cube
cube^M

sphere
sphère^F

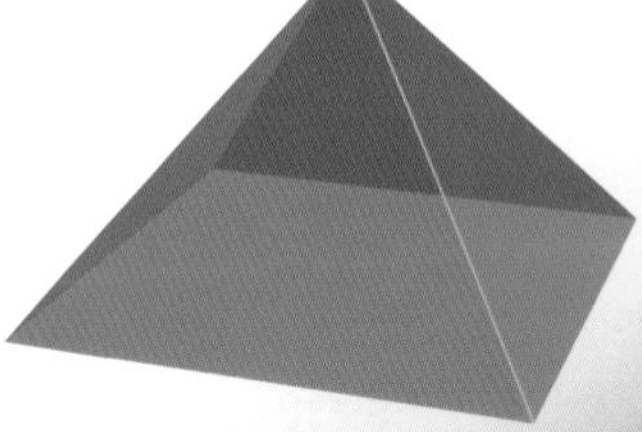

pyramid
pyramide^F

easel
chevalet^M

Numbers and letters
Les chiffres et les lettres

one
un^{M}

two
deux^{M}

three
trois^{M}

four
quatre^{M}

five
cinq^{M}

six
six^{M}

seven
sept^{M}

eight
huit^{M}

nine
neuf^{M}

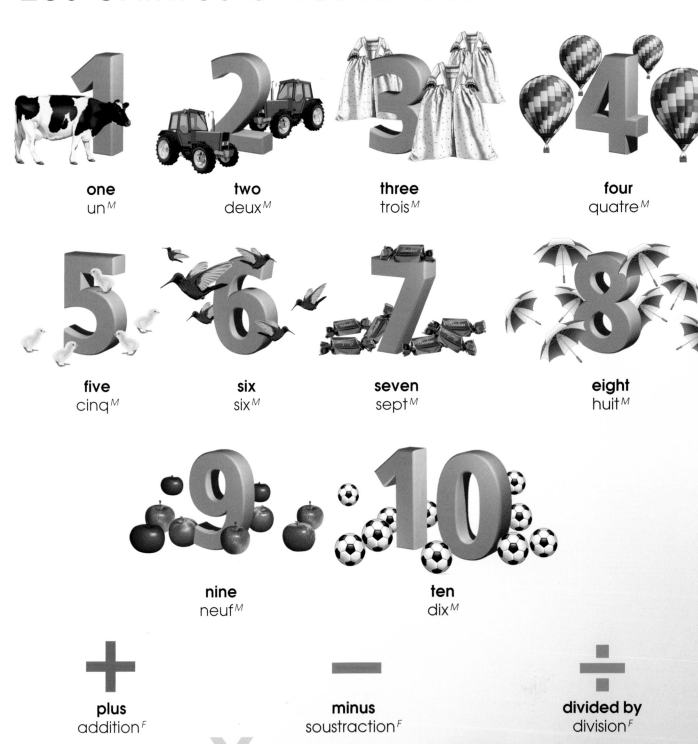

ten
dix^{M}

$+$

plus
addition^{F}

$-$

minus
soustraction^{F}

$\div$

divided by
division^{F}

$\times$

multiplied by
multiplication^{F}

$=$

equals
égale

alphabet
alphabet^{M}

Aa Bb Cc Dd Ee
Ff Gg Hh Ii Jj Kk
Ll Mm Nn Oo Pp
Qq Rr Ss Tt Uu Vv
Ww Xx Yy Zz

Music
La musique

saxophone
saxophone^{M}

key lever
levier^{M} de clé^{F}

reed
anche^{F}

bell
pavillon^{M}

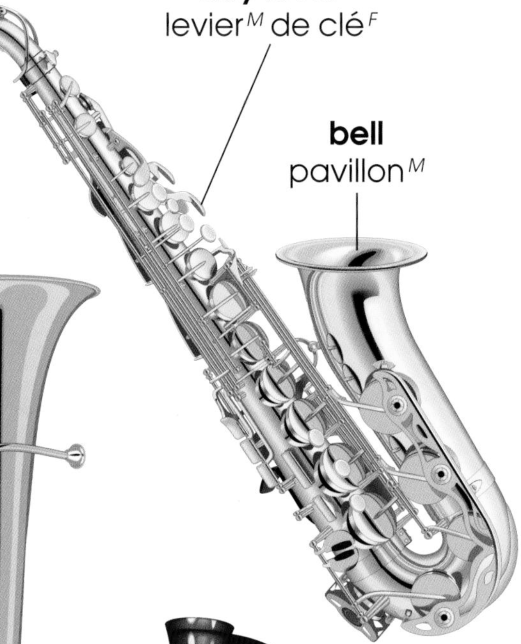

harmonica
harmonica^{M}

accordion
accordéon^{M}

trumpet
trompette^{F}

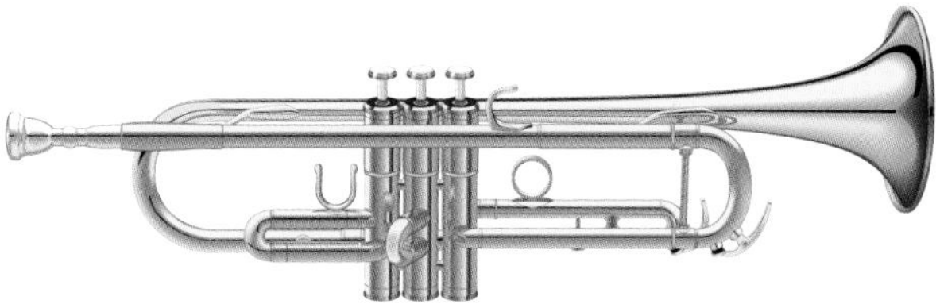

tuba
tuba^{M}

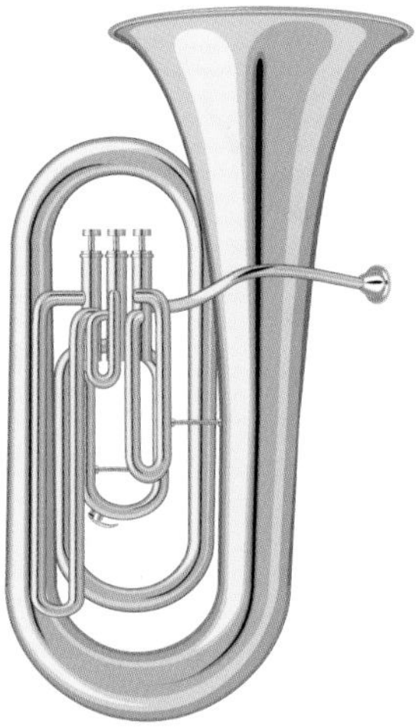

metronome
métronome^{M}

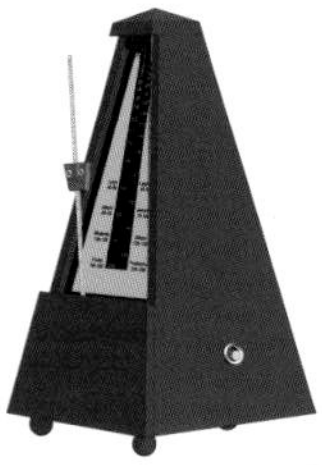

synthesizer
synthétiseur^{M}

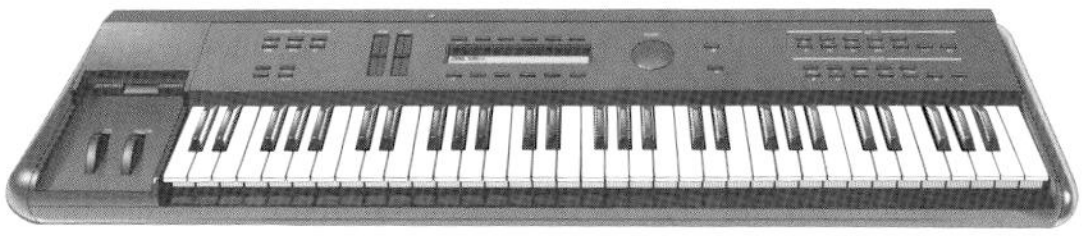

piano
piano^{M}

keyboard
clavier^{M}

pedals
pédales^{F}

transverse flute
flûte^{F} traversière

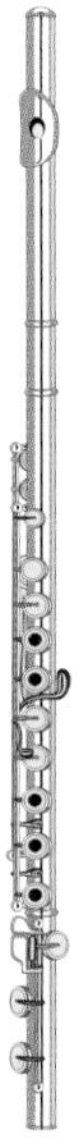

clarinet
clarinette^{F}

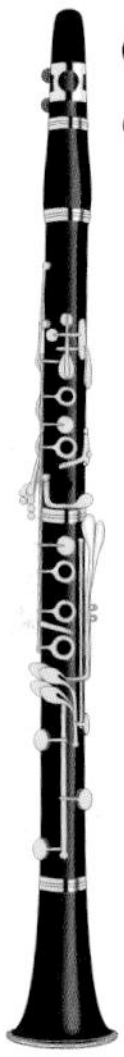

harp
harpe^{F}

recorder
flûte^{F} à bec^{M}

drums
batterie F

xylophone
xylophone M

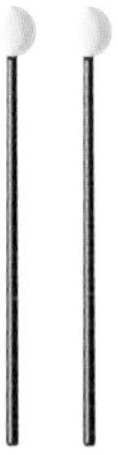

mallets
mailloches F

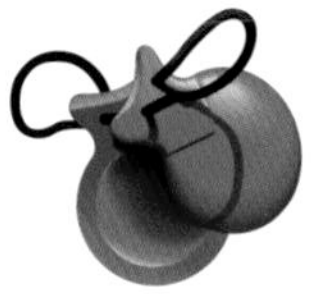

castanets
castagnettes F

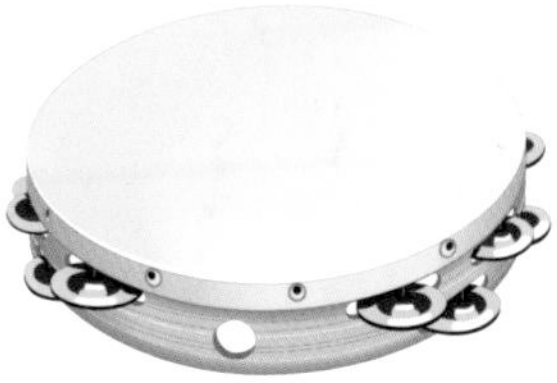

tambourine
tambourin M

drum sticks
baguettes F

triangle
triangle M

cymbals
cymbales F

peg
cheville F

neck
manche M

sound box
caisse F de résonance F

acoustic guitar
guitare F acoustique

plectrum
médiator M

electric guitar
guitare F électrique

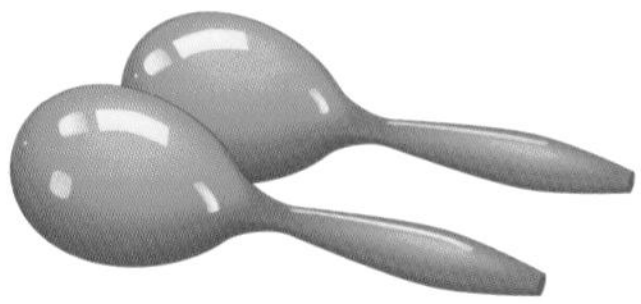

maracas
maracas M

sleigh bells
grelots M

music stand
pupitre M à musique F

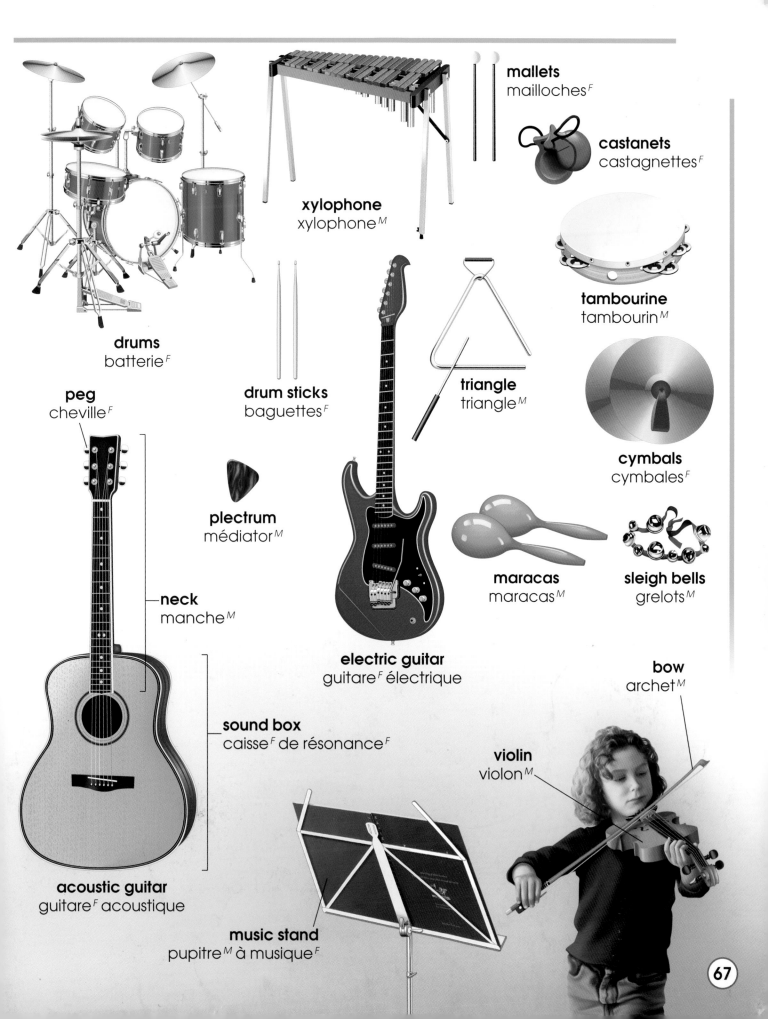

bow
archet M

violin
violon M

Sports
Les sports

bowling ball
boule^F de quilles^F

pin
quille^F

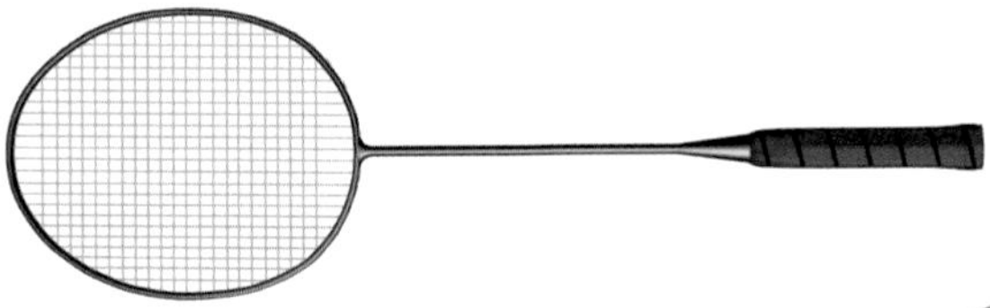

badminton racket
raquette^F de badminton^M

skateboard
planche^F à roulettes^F

shuttlecock
volant^M

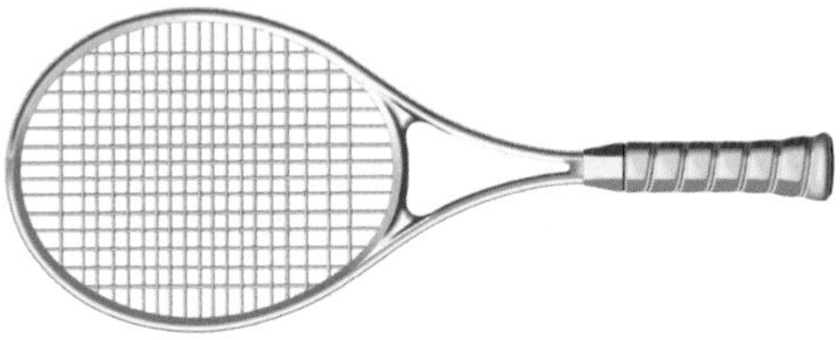

tennis racket
raquette^F de tennis^M

tennis ball
balle^F de tennis^M

table tennis paddle
raquette^F de tennis^M de table^F

goal
but^M

baseball
balle^F de baseball^M

baseball glove
gant^M de baseball^M

in-line skate
patin^M à roues^F alignées

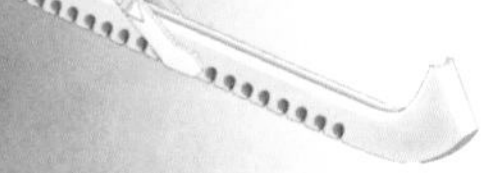

skate guard
protège-lame^M

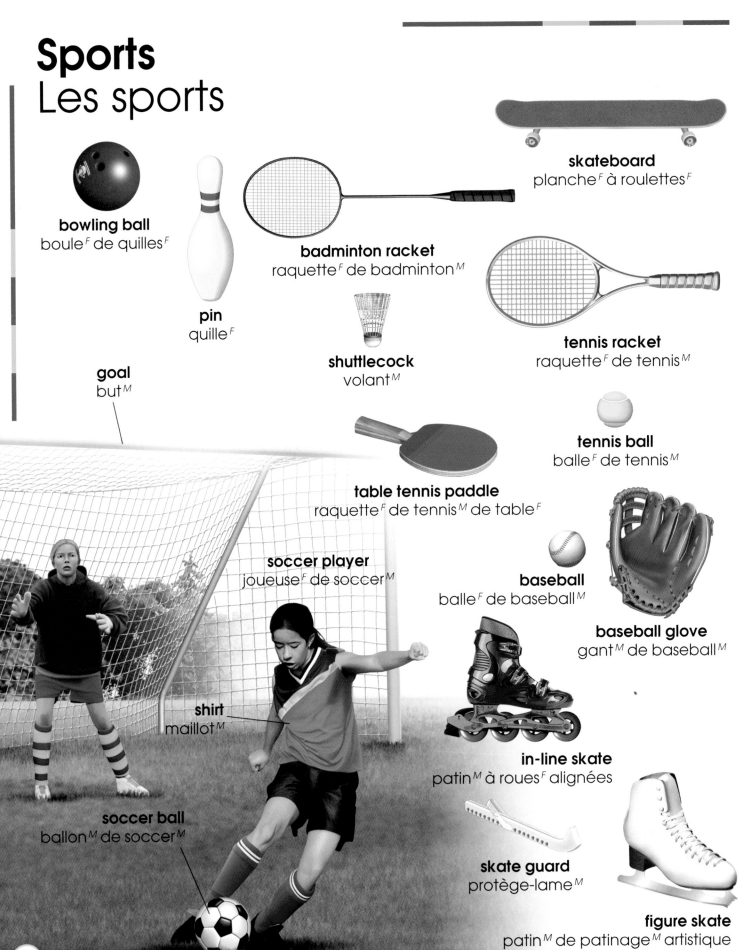

figure skate
patin^M de patinage^M artistique

snowboard
planche^{F} à neige^{F}

cross-country skier
skieur^{M} de fond^{M}

basketball
ballon^{M} de basket^{M}

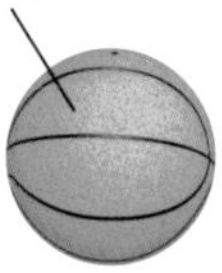

basket
panier^{M}

alpine skier
skieur^{M} alpin

hockey player
joueur^{M} de hockey^{M}

helmet
casque^{M}

stick
bâton^{M}

karateka
karatéka^{F}

swimmer
nageur^{M}

sprinter
sprinteuse^{F}

football player
footballeur^{M}

football
ballon^{M} de football^{M}

golf ball
balle^{F} de golf^{M}

golf club
bâton^{M} de golf^{M}

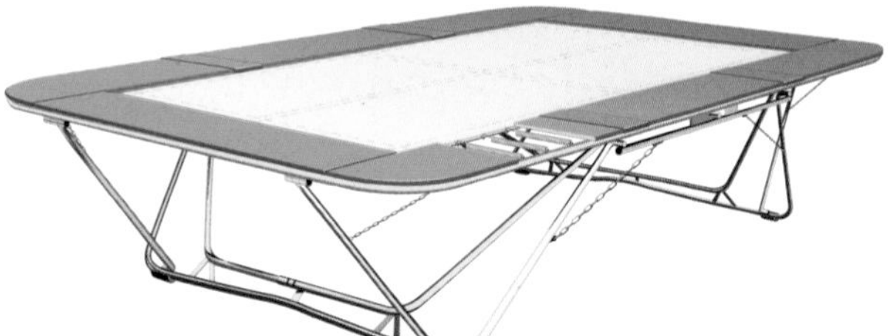

trampoline
trampoline^{M}

Camping
Le camping

Swiss Army knife
couteau^{M} suisse

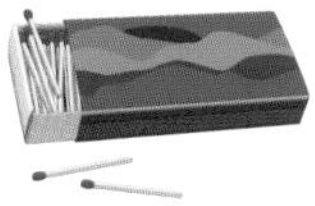

matchbox
boîte^{F} d'allumettes^{F}

cutlery set
ustensiles^{M} de campeur^{M}

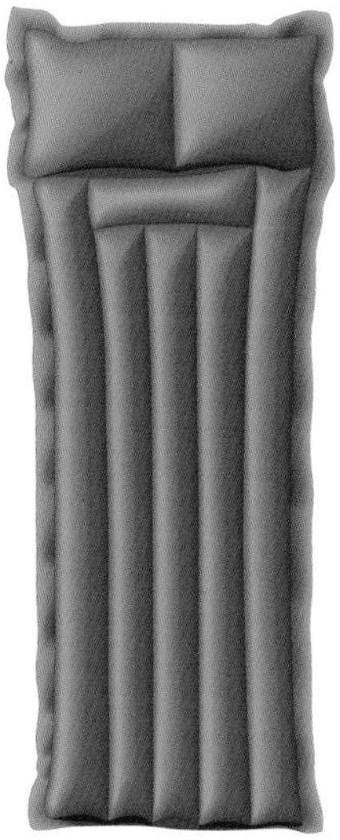

air mattress
matelas^{M} pneumatique

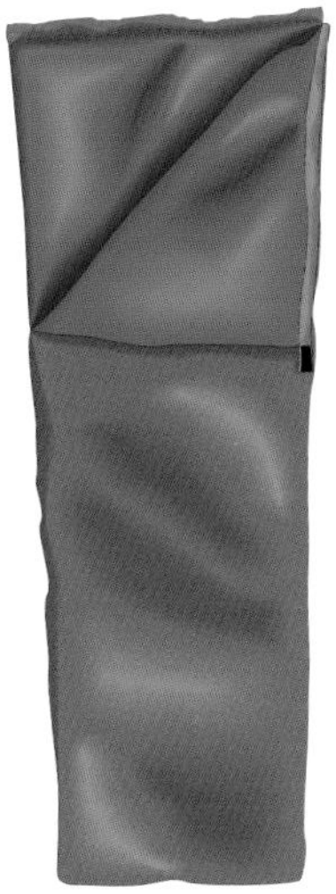

sleeping bag
sac^{M} de couchage^{M}

foam pad
matelas^{M} mousse^{F}

inflator
gonfleur^{M}

cup
tasse^{F}

vacuum bottle
bouteille^{F} isolante

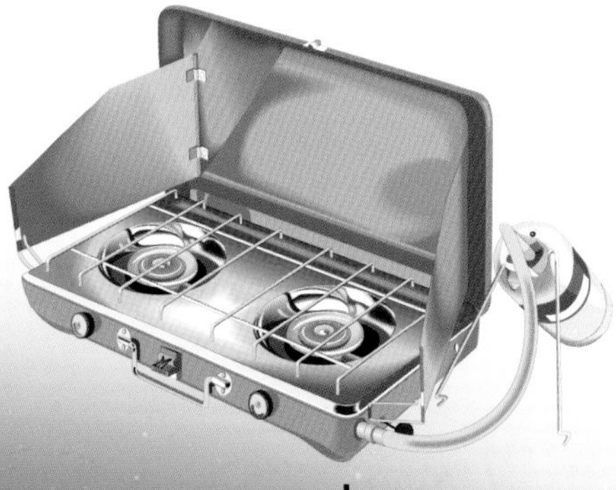

camp stove
réchaud^{M}

frying pan
poêle^{F} à frire

plate
assiette^{F}

campfire
feu^{M} de camp^{M}

lantern
lanterne^{F}

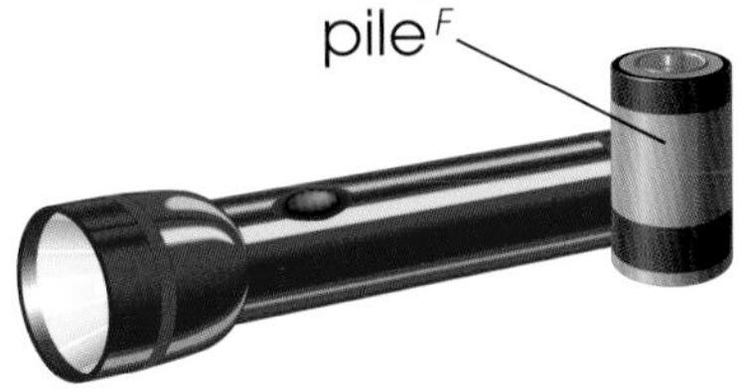

battery
pile^{F}

flashlight
lampe^{F} de poche^{F}

water carrier
cruche^{F}

tent trailer
tente^{F}-caravane^{F}

folding armchair
fauteuil^{M} pliant

cooler
glacière^{F}

trailer
caravane^{F}

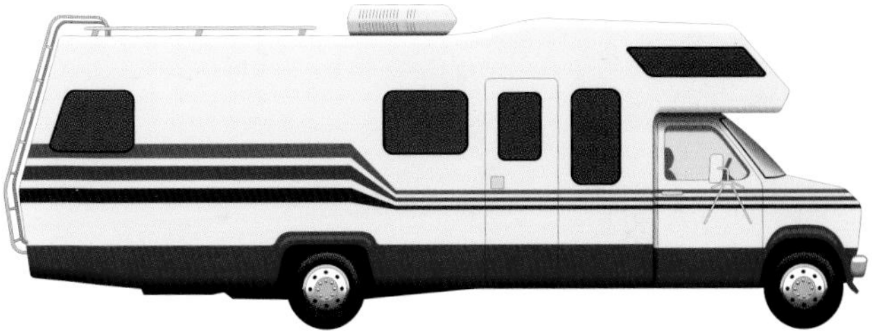

motor home
auto^{F}-caravane^{F}

picnic table
table^{F} de pique-nique^{M}

tent
tente^{F}

rainfly
double toit^{M}

stake
piquet^{M}

door
porte^{F}

Parties and holidays
Les fêtes

birthday cake
gâteau^{M} d'anniversaire^{M}

candle
bougie^{F}

confetti
confettis^{M}

streamers
serpentins^{M}

crackers
pétards^{M}

gift wrap
papier^{M} d'emballage^{M}

balloon
ballon^{M}

greeting card
carte^{F} de vœux^{M}

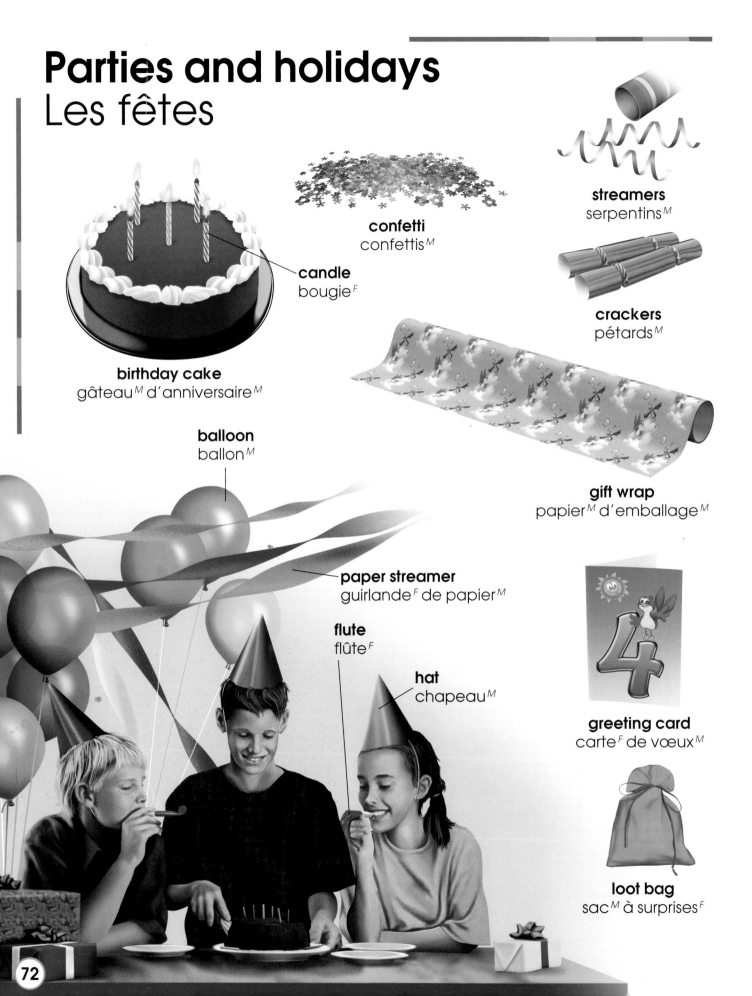

loot bag
sac^{M} à surprises^{F}

fireworks
feu^M d'artifice^M

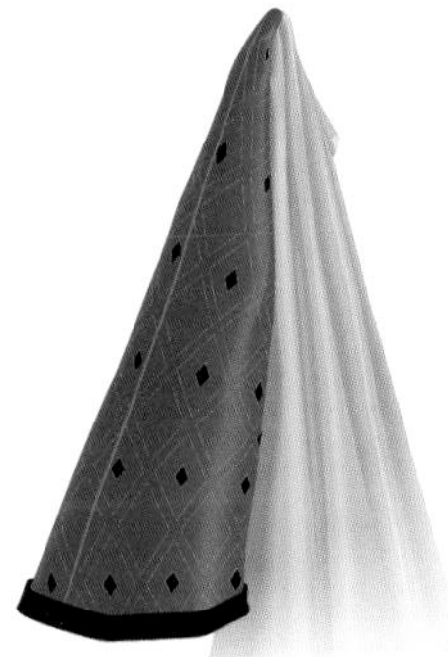

headdress
hennin^M

mask
masque^M

Easter eggs
œufs^M de Pâques^F

ribbon
ruban^M

gift
cadeau^M

piñata
piñata^F

gift bag
sac^M cadeau^M

Halloween pumpkin
citrouille^F d'Halloween^F

star
étoile^F

garland
guirlande^F

ball
boule^F

Christmas tree
arbre^M de Noël^M

Costumes and characters
Les costumes et les personnages

magician
magicien [M]

juggler
jongleur [M]

monster
monstre [M]

princess
princesse [F]

king
roi [M]

gnome
gnome [M]

robot
robot [M]

witch
sorcière [F]

fairy
fée [F]

sleigh
traîneau [M]

reindeer
renne [M]

Santa Claus
père [M] Noël [M]

ghost
fantôme [M]

knight
chevalier^M

Gallic warrior
guerrier^M gaulois

soldier
soldat^M

Roman legionary
légionnaire^M romain

pirate
pirate^M

cowboy
cowboy^M

Native American
Amérindienne^F

ballerina
ballerine^F

trainer
dompteur^M

dragon
dragon^M

clown
clown^M

English Index

A

abacus 65
abdomen 4
above-ground swimming pool 11
accordion 66
acoustic guitar 67
adhesive bandage 14
adhesive tape 19
afraid 7
air mattress 70
airplane 52
alarm clock 12
alfalfa sprouts 25
alga 38
allosaurus 40
alphabet 65
alpine skier 69
aluminum foil 28
anchor 51
angry 7
ankle 4
ankylosaurus 40
anorak 8
ant 31
antelope 37
apple 26
apricot 26
apron 20
arm 4
armchair 16
artichoke 24
asparagus 24
assembly toy 18
asteroid belt 44
astronaut 59
autumn 48
avocado 25

B

baby food 28
back of the hand 4
backhoe loader 58
backpack 60
bacon 29
bactrian camel 36
badminton racket 68
bag 58
bag of cookies 28
bagel 28
baggage trailer 52
baguette 28
baking sheet 21
ball 11, 73
ballerina 75
balloon 72
ballpoint pen 61
banana 26
barley 33
barn 33
barrette 15
base 16
baseball 68
baseball glove 68
basket 53, 69
basketball 69
bathroom scale 14
bathtub 14
battery 71
beach 46
beach towel 38
beach umbrella 39
bean 25
bear 35
beaver 35
bedside table 13
beet 24
behind 7
bell 66
bell tower 56
belt 9
beside 7
bicycle 54
bicycle helmet 54
biplane 53
birch 34
bird feeder 43
birdhouse 43
birthday cake 72
black currants 27
blackberries 27
blackboard eraser 60
blender 20
blocks 18
blue 62
blue + red = purple 62
blueberries 26
blusher 15
boat 50
bobby pin 15
bone 5, 31
book 17
bookcase 17
boot 9
bow 50, 67
bowl 31
bowling ball 68
boxer shorts 9
brachiosaurus 40
brake 54
branch 30
branches 34
briefs 9
broccoli 24
brown sugar 23
brush 19
brussels sprouts 24
bubble bath 14
bucket 38
bucket swing 11
bud 43
budgie 30
bulletin board 60
bumblebee 31
bun 23
bus shelter 57
bush 42
business aircraft 53
butte 47
butter 28
butter dish 22
butterfly 31
butterfly fish 38
button 9

C

cabbage 24
cabinet 20
cage 30
cake 23
calculator 60
calf 33
camp stove 70
campfire 70
can opener 21
canary 30
candies 29
candle 72
canoe 51
car 55
car wash 57
carambola 27
caravel 51
cardigan 8
cards 19
cargo aircraft 53
carnation 42
carrot 24
cash register 28
cassette 13
cassette player 17
castanets 67
cat 30
catamaran 50
cauliflower 24
cave 47
CD-radio-cassette player 13
CD/DVD drive 61
ceiling fixture 13
celery 24
cereal 23
chair 60
chalk 60
chalk board 60
chameleon 30
changing table 12
cheese 28
cherries 27
chick 32
chicken 29
chiffonier 13
child carrier 54
child safety seat 54
chimney 11
chin 4
chipmunk 35
chives 25
chocolate bar 29
Christmas tree 73
chrysalis 31
church 56
cicada 31
circle 63
citrus juicer 21
city bus 55
clarinet 66
claw 36
cliff 46
clip 60
clock 60
cloud 49
cloud of volcanic ash 47
clown 75
clown fish 38
coat hooks 13
coconut 27
coffeemaker 20
colander 20
collar 9
colored pencils 19
comb 15
comet 45
comforter 12
compact disc 13, 61
compact disc player 17
compost bin 43
compressed-air cylinder 59
computer 61
condominiums 56
cone 63
confetti 72
container ship 51
control tower 52
controller 19
cooked ham 29
cookie cutters 21
cookies 23
cooler 71
corkscrew 21
corn 33
corncob 33
cotton applicators 14
counter 29
cow 32
cowboy 75
crab 39
crackers 72
cranberry 27
crater 47
crawl 6
crayons 19
creamer 22
crescent moon 44
crib 12
crocodile 37
crocus 42
croissant 28
cross-country skier 69
cry 7
cube 63
cucumber 25
cup 22, 70
curling iron 15
currant 27
curtain 12
cushion 16
cutlery set 70
cutting board 21
cylinder 63
cymbals 67

D

daffodil 42
daisy 42
dandelion 42
darts 19
deer 35
deinonychus 40
dental floss 14
desert 47
dew 48
die 19
diplodocus 41
dishwasher 20
diskette 61
diskette drive 61
disposable razor 15
divided by 64
dog 31
doll 18
dolphin 39
dominoes 19
donkey 32
door 11, 13, 71
down 7
dragon 75
dragonfly 31
drawer 20
drawing board 18
dress 8
dresser 12
drive chain 54
driver 58
drizzle 49
dromedary camel 36
drum sticks 67
drums 67
dryer 15
duck 32
dune 47
duty belt 59
DVD 17
DVD player 17

E

ear 4
Earth 44
easel 19, 63
Easter eggs 73
edger 10
egg 28
egg carton 28
eggplant 25
eight 64
elbow 4
electric guitar 67
electric range 21
electric razor 15
elephant 37
engine 52
equals 64
eraser 61
eraser holder 61
eye 4, 48
eyelash 4
eyelid 4
eyeshadow 15

F

factory 57
fairy 74
falcon 35
fan 16
faucet 14
felt tip pen 19
fence 10
fennec 36
fennel 24
fern 34
field mouse 35
fig 27
figure skate 68
finger 4
fingernail 4
fins 38
fir 34
fire extinguisher 59
fire hose 59
fire hydrant 57
fire irons 17
fire station 56
fire truck 59
fire-fighting aircraft 53
firefighter 59
fireplace 16
fireworks 73
fish 23
five 64
flashlight 71
flat sheet 12
fleshy leaf 25
floor lamp 16
flour 23
flower 43
flower bud 43
flute 72
fly 8, 31
foam pad 70
fog 48
folding armchair 71
folding chairs 16
foliage 34
food can 28
foot 4
football 69
football player 69
footboard 12
fork 23, 33
fountain pen 61
four 64
freezer 20
freezer bag 28
freezing rain 49
frog 35
frost 49
fruit juice 28
frying pan 21, 70
full moon 44
funnel 21
funnel cloud 48
fuselage 52
futon 16

G

galaxy 45
galley 51
Gallic warrior 75
game console 19
garage 11
garbage can 10
garden hose 10
gardening gloves 43
garland 73
garlic 25
gasoline pump 57
geographical map 60
gherkin 25
ghost 74
gift 73
gift bag 73
gift wrap 72
giraffe 37
glacier 46
glass 22
glider swing 11
globe 60
gloves 9
glue stick 19
gnome 74
goal 68
goat 32
goldfinch 35
goldfish 30
golf ball 69
golf club 69
goose 32
gorilla 37
grandfather clock 16
grapefruit 26
grapes 27
grasshopper 31
grater 21
gravy boat 22
green 62
green peas 25
greeting card 72
guinea pig 30
gull 39
gum 5

H

hadrosaurus 40
hail 49
hair dryer 15
hairbrush 15
Halloween pumpkin 73
hammer 10
hamster 30
hand mixer 20
handlebars 54
hanger 12
hard hat 58
hare 35
harmonica 66
harp 66
hat 72
hatchet 59
head 4
headboard 12
headdress 73
headlight 55
headphones 17
heart 5
heavy rain 49
hedge 11
heel 8
helicopter 53
helmet 59, 69
hen 32
hen house 32
high-rise apartment building 56
highlighter pen 61

highway crossing 54
hill 46
hippopotamus 37
hive 33
hockey player 69
honey 23
honeybee 33
honeycomb 33
honeydew melon 26
hood 55
hoof 32
horse 32
horseshoe 32
hose trolley 10
hot-air balloon 53
hotel 56
hovercraft 50
Hubble space telescope 44
hyena 37

I

ice breaker 50
ice cream 23
ice cream cup 28
ice-cream scoop 21
in 7
in front of 7
in-ground swimming pool 11
in-line skate 68
index finger 5
inflator 70
interlocking blocks 18
international space station 45
intestines 5
iris 4

J

jar 30
jay 35
jeans 8
jerboa 36
jewel box 12
juggler 74
jump 6
Jupiter 44

K

kangaroo 36
karateka 69
kayak 51
kennel 31
ketchup 29
kettle 20
key lever 66
keyboard 61, 66
king 74
kitchen knife 21
kitchen timer 21
kiwi 27
knee 4
knife 22
knight 75
knit shirt 8
knitted cap 9

L

ladybug 31
lake 46
lantern 71
larva 31
laugh 7
laundry basket 13
lava flow 47
lawn 10
lawn rake 10
leaf 43
leeks 25
leg 4
lemon 26
leopard 37
letter 58
lettuce 24
life buoy 51
light aircraft 53
lighthouse 51
lightning 49
lily 42
lily of the valley 42
lime 26
linen chest 13
lion 37
lip 5
lipstick 15
litchi 27
little finger 5
lizard 36
lobster 29
locomotive 55
log carrier 17
loose-leaf paper 61
loot bag 72
love seat 16
lungs 5

M

magician 74
magma 47
mail carrier 58
main vent 47
mallets 67
mane 32
mango 27
maple 34
maple syrup 23
maracas 67
marker 61
Mars 44
mask 38, 59, 73
mast 50
matchbox 70
measuring cup 21
measuring spoons 21
mechanical pencil 61
medicine cabinet 14
memo pad 19
Mercury 44
meteorite 45
metronome 66
microwave oven 20
middle finger 5
milk carton 28
millet 33
mini stereo sound system 17
minivan 55
minus 64
mirror 12
mist 48
mitten 9
mixed forest 46
mixing bowls 20
mobile 12
modeling clay 18
mongoose 37
monitor 19
monster 74
Moon 44
moose 35
motor home 71
motor scooter 54
motorcycle 54
motorcycle helmet 54
mountain 46
mouse 61
mouth 5
mouthwash 14
mower 10
muffin pan 21
multiplied by 64
muscle 5
mushroom 34
music box 12
music stand 67
muskmelon 26
mussel 29

N

nail clippers 14
nail enamel 15
napkin 22
Native American 75
navel 4
neck 4, 67
necktie 9
nectarine 26
Neptune 45
new moon 44
nine 64
nose 4, 52
notebook 61
nuts 27

O

oak 34
oasis 47
oats 33
octopus 39
olive oil 29
olives 25
on 7
one 64
one-storey house 56
onion 25
orange 26, 62
orchid 42
ostrich 32
ottoman 16
oval 63
oven 21
oven mitt 20
overalls 8
overhead projector 60
owl 35
ox 33
oyster 29

P

pachycephalosaurus 40
paddle 51
pajamas 9
palm of the hand 5
palm tree 39
papaya 27
paper clips 60
paper punch 60
paper streamer 72
parallelogram 63
parasaurolophus 41
park 57
parrot 30
parsnip 24
passenger transfer vehicle 52
passion fruit 27
pasta 28
path 42
peach 26
pear 26
pedal 54
pedals 66
pedestrian crossing 57
peeler 21
peg 67
peg puzzle 18
pelican 39
pencil 61
pencil sharpener 61
pepper mill 23
perfume 15
personal flotation device 51
personal stereo 13
personal watercraft 51
petal 42
physician 58
piano 66
pick 33
pickup truck 55
picnic table 71
pie 23
pie pan 21
pig 32
pigeon 31
pillow 12
pin 68
piñata 73
pine 34
pineapple 27
pinecone 34
pirate 75
pita bread 28
pizza 23
planetarium 44
plant 43
plastic film (cellophane) 28
plate 23, 70
plateau 46
playpen 12
playset 11
plectrum 67
plums 26
plus 64
Pluto 45
pocket 9
police car 59
police officer 59
police station 56
pomegranate 27
pond 42
poplar 34
poppy 42
porcupine 35
poster 12
potatoes 24
potty 15
pouch 36
princess 74
printer 61
protractor 60
prune 27
pruning shears 43
pulp 27
pupil 4
purple 62
pyramid 63

Q

quail 32
quarter moon 44

R

rabbit 30
racing car 58
radish 24
railroad track 54
rain 49
rainbow 48
raindrop 49
rainfly 71
raisin 27
rake 10
ramekin 22
raspberries 27
rat 30
rattle 18
rattlesnake 36
recorder 66
rectangle 63
red 62
reed 66
refrigerator 20
reindeer 74
remote control 17
restaurant 56
rhamphorynchus 41
rhinoceros 37
rhombus 63
rhubarb 24
ribbon 73
rice 28
rime 48
rind 27
ring binder 61
river estuary 46
road worker 58
roadwork 57
robin 35
robot 74
rocket 44
rocking chair 13
rocking horse 18
rolling pin 21
Roman legionary 75
roof 11
rooster 32
root 25, 34, 43
rose 42
rug 12
ruler 61
run 6
running shoe 8
rutabaga 24

S

sail 50
sailboat 50
salad 23
salad bowl 22
salad spinner 20
salami 29
salmon 29
salt shaker 23
sand castle 38
sandal 8
sandbox 11
sandwich 23
Santa Claus 74
satellite 45
Saturn 45
saucepan 21
sausage 29
saxophone 66
scale 58
scale leaf 25
scarf 9
school bus 55
school zone 57
scissors 19
scorpion 36
scouring pad 21
scream 7
screwdriver 10
scythe 33
sea 46
sea horse 39
sea urchin 38
seal 38
seaplane 53
seashells 38
seat 54
section of an apple 26
section of an orange 27
seed 26
segment 27
semidetached house 56
service station 57
seven 64
shade 16
shampoo 14
shark 38
shed 10
sheep 32
shirt 9, 68
shoelace 8
shopping basket 29
shopping cart 29
shoreline 46
shorts 9
shoulder 4
shovel 38
shower curtain 14
shuttlecock 68
sidewalk 57
silo 33
sink 14, 20
sit 6
six 64
skate 39
skate guard 68
skateboard 68
skin 26
skirt 8
skunk 35
skyscraper 57
sleep 6
sleeping bag 70
sleet 49
sleeve 9
sleigh 74
sleigh bells 67
slide 6, 11
slipper 13
small decanter 22
small hand cultivator 43
smile 7
snake 35
snow 49
snowboard 69
snowflake 49
snowsuit 9
soap 14
soccer ball 68
soccer player 68
soccer table 19
socks 9
sofa 16
sofa bed 16
soldier 75
sole 8
sound box 67
soup bowl 22
soup tureen 22
soybean sprouts 25
space probe 45
space shuttle 45
spade 43
spaghetti 23
spaghetti squash 25
sparrow 35
speaker 17, 61
speedboat 51
sphere 63
spices 28
spider 31
spider web 31
spinach 24
spinning top 18
spinosaurus 41
spiral notebook 61
sponge 14
spoon 22
spouted cup 22
spring 48
sprinkler 10
sprinter 69
spruce 34
square 63

squirrel 35
stackable rings 18
stake 71
stapler 60
staples 60
star 73
starfish 38
steak 23, 29
stegosaurus 40
stem 26, 43
stepladder 10
stern 50
stethoscope 58
stew 23
stick 69
stock pot 21
stomach 5
stop 57
store 56
strap 8
strawberries 26
streamers 72
street 57
streetcar 55
stroller 18
student 60
student's desk 60
submarine 50
subway train 55
sucker 39
sugar 23
sugar bowl 22
summer 48
summit 46
Sun 44
sunflower 42
sunglasses 38
sunscreen 38
surface element 21
surfboard 38
surprised 7
sweatpants 9
sweatshirt 9
sweet pepper 25
sweet potato 24
swimmer 69
swimming trunks 9
swimsuit 9
swing 11
Swiss Army knife 70
synthesizer 66

T

T-shirt 8
table 16
table lamp 12
table tennis paddle 68
tablecloth 22
tail 32, 52
tambourine 67
tanker 50
tarantula 36
tea towel 21
teapot 22
teddy bear 12
telephone 17
telescope 44
television set 17
ten 64
tennis ball 68
tennis racket 68
tent 71
tent trailer 71
tentacle 39
thermometer 49
third finger 5
thistle 42
thorax 4
three 64
thumb 5
thumb tacks 60
tick 36
tiger 37
tire 55
tissues 14
toaster 20
toe 4
toilet 14
toilet paper 14
tomato 25
tongue 5, 8
tool box 10
tooth 5
toothbrush 14
toothpaste 14
tornado 48
tortillas 28
tow tractor 52
towel 15
toy cars 18
toy garage 18
toy train 18
tractor 32
traffic lights 57
trailer 71
train 55
trainer 75
trampoline 69
transverse flute 66
trapeze 11
trapezoid 63
tree 34
triangle 60, 63, 67
triceratops 41
tricycle 11
tropical cyclone 48
tropical forest 46
trowel 43
trumpet 66
trunk 34, 37, 55
tuba 66
tulip 42
tundra 46
tunnel 6
turkey 23, 32
turnip 24
turtle 30
turtleneck 8
tusk 37
two 64
tyrannosaurus 41

U

under 7
universal step 52
up 7
Uranus 45

V

vacuum bottle 70
valley 46
vegetable garden 10
Venus 44
video entertainment system 19
video monitor 61
videocassette 17
videocassette recorder (VCR) 17
violin 67
vivarium 30
volcano 47
vulture 36

W

wagon 11
walk 6
walker 18
wardrobe 13
washcloth 15
washer 15
water carrier 71
water pitcher 22
watercolor paints 19
watering can 43
watermelon 27
whale 39
wheat 33
wheelbarrow 10
white + black = gray 62
white bread 28
window 11, 52, 55
windshield 55
wine vinegar 29
wineglass 22
wing 52
winter 48
witch 74
wolf 35
woodpecker 35
workbench 18
wrist 4

X

xylophone 67

Y

yacht 51
yellow 62
yellow + blue = green 62
yellow + red = orange 62
yogurt 28

Z

zebra 37
zest 27
zucchini 25

Index français

A

à côté 7
abat-jour 16
abeille 33
abribus 57
abricot 26
accessoires de foyer 17
accordéon 66
addition 64
aéroglisseur 50
affiche 12
agent de police 59
agrafes 60
agrafeuse 60
ail 25
aile 52
algue 38
allée 42
allosaure 40
alphabet 65
Amérindienne 75
ananas 27
anche 66
ancre 51
âne 32
ankylosaure 40
anneaux à empiler 18
annulaire 5
anorak 8
antilope 37
appartements en copropriété 56
araignée 31
arbre 34
arbre de Noël 73
arbuste 42
arc-en-ciel 48
archet 67
armoire 20
armoire-penderie 13
arrêt 57
arroseur 10
arrosoir 43
artichaut 24
asperge 24
assiette 23, 70
astronaute 59
aubergine 25
auriculaire 5
auto-caravane 71
autobus 55
autobus scolaire 55
automne 48
autruche 32
avion 52
avion d'affaires 53
avion léger 53
avion-cargo 53
avion-citerne 53
avocat 25
avoine 33
avoir peur 7

B

babillard 60
baby-foot 19
bac à compost 43
bac à sable 11
bacon 29
bagel 28
baguette 28
baguettes 67
baignoire 14
bain moussant 14
baladeur 13
balai à feuilles 10
balancelle double 11
balançoire 11
baleine 39
balle de baseball 68
balle de golf 69
balle de tennis 68
ballerine 75
ballon 11, 72
ballon de basket 69
ballon de football 69
ballon de soccer 68
banane 26
barrette 15
bassin 42
bateau 50
bâton 69
bâton de golf 69
bâtonnet de colle 19
batterie 67
batteur à main 20
bêche 43
berceuse 13
berlingot de lait 28
betterave 24
beurre 28
beurrier 22
bibliothèque 17
bicyclette 54
bifteck 29
biplan 53
biscuits 23
blanc + noir = gris 62
blé 33
bleu 62
bleu + rouge = violet 62
bleuets 26
bloc-notes 19
bocal 30
boîte à musique 12
boîte à outils 10
boîte à œufs 28
boîte d'allumettes 70
boîte de conserve 28
bol 22, 31
bols à mélanger 20
bonbons 29
borne d'incendie 57
botte 9
bouche 5
bouée de sauvetage 51
bougie 72
bouilloire 20
boule 73
boule de quilles 68
bouleau 34
boulier 65
bourdon 31
bourgeon 43
bouteille d'air comprimé 59
bouteille isolante 70
bouton 9
bouton floral 43
bœuf 33
brachiosaure 40
braguette 8
branche 30
bras 4
bretelle 8
brioche 23
briques 18
brise-glace 50
brocoli 24
brosse 15, 60
brosse à dents 14
brouette 10
brouillard 48
bruine 49
brume 48
bureau d'élève 60
but 68
butte 47

C

cadeau 73
cafetière 20
cage 30
cahier 61
caille 32
caisse de résonance 67
caisse enregistreuse 28
calculatrice 60
caleçon 9
caméléon 30
camion d'incendie 59
camionnette 55
canapé 16
canapé convertible 16
canard 32
canneberge 27
canot 51
capot 55
carafon 22
carambole 27
caravane 71
caravelle 51
cardigan 8
carotte 24
carré 63
carte de vœux 72
carte géographique 60
cartes 19
caserne de pompiers 56
casque 59, 69
casque d'écoute 17
casque de moto 54
casque de sécurité 58
casque de vélo 54
casse-tête 18
casserole 21
cassette 13
cassette vidéo 17
cassis 27
cassonade 23
castagnettes 67
castor 35
causeuse 16
ceinture 9
ceinture d'astéroïdes 44
ceinturon de service 59
céleri 24
centre d'activités 11
cercle 63
céréales 23
cerises 27
chaîne 54
chaise 60
chaises pliantes 16
chameau 36
champignon 34
chapeau 72
chardon 42
chardonneret 35
chariot 29
chariot à bagages 52
chat 30
château de sable 38
chaussettes 9
chaussure de sport 8
cheminée 11, 47
chemise 9
chêne 34

chenille 31
cheval 32
cheval à bascule 18
chevalet 19, 63
chevalier 75
cheville 4, 67
chèvre 32
chevreuil 35
chien 31
chiffonnier 13
chou 24
chou-fleur 24
choux de Bruxelles 24
chrysalide 31
ciboulette 25
cigale 31
cil 4
cinq 64
cintre 12
ciseaux 19
citron 26
citrouille d'Halloween 73
clarinette 66
clavier 61, 66
clocher 56
clôture 10
clown 75
coccinelle 31
cochon d'Inde 30
coffre 13, 55
coffret à bijoux 12
col 9
col roulé 8
colline 46
comète 45
commode 12
comptoir vitré 29
concombre 25
cône 34, 63
confettis 72
congélateur 20
console de jeu 19
coq 32
coquelicot 42
coquillages 38
cornichon 25
coton-tige 14
cou 4
coude 4
coulée de lave 47
couleuvre 35
coupe d'une orange 27
coupe d'une pomme 26
coupe-ongles 14
courge spaghetti 25
courgette 25
courir 6
coussin 16
couteau 22
couteau de cuisine 21
couteau suisse 70
cowboy 75
cœur 5
crabe 39
craie 60
cratère 47
cravate 9
crayon 61
crayons de cire 19
crayons de couleur 19
crème glacée 23
crémier 22
crier 7
crinière 32
crocodile 37
crocus 42
croissant 28, 44
cruche 71
cube 63
cubes 18
cuiller 22
cuiller à crème glacée 21
cuillers doseuses 21
cuisinière électrique 21
cyclone tropical 48
cylindre 63
cymbales 67

D

dans 7
dauphin 39
dé 19
débarbouillette 15
défense 37
deinonychus 40
dent 5
dentifrice 14
derrière 7
désert 47
deux 64
devant 7
dévidoir sur roues 10
dinde 23
dindon 32
diplodocus 41
disque compact 13, 61
disquette 61
distributeur d'essence 57
division 64
dix 64
doigt 4
dominos 19
dompteur 75
dormir 6
dos de la main 4
double toit 71
dragon 75
drap 12
dromadaire 36
dune 47
DVD 17

E

écaille 25
éclair 49
écorce 27
écran 19, 61
écran solaire 38
écureuil 35
édredon 12
égale 64
église 56
éléphant 37
élève 60
emporte-pièces 21
en bas 7
en haut 7
entonnoir 21
épaule 4
épi de maïs 33
épices 28
épinard 24
épinette 34
éplucheur 21
éponge 14
éponge à récurer 21
équerre 60
érable 34
escabeau 10
escalier d'accès 52
essoreuse à salade 20
estomac 5
estuaire 46
établi 18
été 48
étoile 73
étoile de mer 38
être assis 6
être fâché 7
être surpris 7
évier 20
extincteur 59

F

factrice 58
falaise 46
fantôme 74
fard à joues 15
farine 23
faucon 35
fauteuil 16
fauteuil pliant 71
faux 33
fée 74
fenêtre 11
fennec 36
fenouil 24
fer à cheval 32
fer à friser 15
feu d'artifice 73
feu de camp 70
feu de circulation 57
feuillage 34
feuille 43
feuilles mobiles 61
feutre 19
figue 27
fil dentaire 14
fleur 43
flocon de neige 49
flûte 72
flûte à bec 66
flûte traversière 66
footballeur 69
forêt mixte 46
forêt tropicale 46
fougère 34
foulard 9
four 21
four à micro-ondes 20
fourche 33
fourchette 23
fourgonnette 55
fourmi 31
foyer 16
fraises 26
framboises 27
frein 54
fromages 28
fruit de la Passion 27
fusée 44
fuselage 52
futon 16

G

gadelle 27
galaxie 45
galère 51
gant de baseball 68
gants 9
gants de jardinage 43
garage 11, 18
gâteau 23
gâteau d'anniversaire 72
geai 35
gencive 5
genou 4
gerboise 36
germes de soya 25
gilet de sauvetage 51
girafe 37
givre 48
glace 55
glacier 46
glacière 71
glissoire 6, 11
globe terrestre 60
gnome 74
gobelet à bec 22
goéland 39
gomme 61
gonfleur 70
gorille 37
goutte d'eau 49
grange 33
gratte-ciel 57
grêlon 49
grelots 67
grenade 27
grenouille 35
grésil 49
griffe à fleurs 43
grille-pain 20
grotte 47
guerrier gaulois 75
guidon 54
guirlande 73
guirlande de papier 72
guitare acoustique 67
guitare électrique 67

H

habit de neige 9
hache 59
hadrosaure 40
haie 11
hamster 30
haricot 25
harmonica 66
harpe 66
haut-parleur 17, 61
hélicoptère 53
hennin 73
hibou 35
hippocampe 39
hippopotame 37
hiver 48
hochet 18
homard 29
horloge de parquet 16
hors-bord 51
hôtel 56
hublot 52
huile d'olive 29
huit 64
huître 29
hydravion 53
hyène 37

I

imprimante 61
index 5
intestins 5
iris 4

J

jambe 4
jambon cuit 29
jardin potager 10
jaune 62
jaune + bleu = vert 62
jaune + rouge = orange 62
jean 8
jeu de fléchettes 19
jongleur 74
jonquille 42
joueur de hockey 69
joueuse de soccer 68
jupe 8
Jupiter 44
jus de fruits 28

K

kangourou 36
karatéka 69
kayak 51
ketchup 29
kiwi 27

L

lac 46
lacet 8
laitue 24
lampadaire 16
lampe de poche 71
lampe de table 12
langue 5
languette 8
lanterne 71
lapin 30
lavabo 14
lave-auto 57
lave-vaisselle 20
laveuse 15
lecteur de cassette 17
lecteur de CD/DVD 61
lecteur de disque compact 17
lecteur de disquette 61
lecteur de DVD 17
légionnaire romain 75
léopard 37
lettre 58
levier de clé 66
lèvre 5
lézard 36
libellule 31
lièvre 35
lime 26
lion 37
lis 42
lit à barreaux 12
lit pliant 12
litchi 27
littoral 46
livre 17
locomotive 55
losange 63
loup 35
Lune 44
lunettes de soleil 38
luzerne 25

M

magasin 56
magicien 74
magma 47
magnétoscope 17
mailloches 67
maillot 68
maillot de bain 9
maïs 33
maison d'oiseau 43
maison de plain-pied 56
maison jumelée 56
majeur 5
manche 9, 67
manette de jeu 19
mangeoire 43
mangouste 37
mangue 27
maracas 67
marcher 6
marguerite 42
marmite 21
marqueur 61
Mars 44
marteau 10
masque 38, 59, 73
mât 50
matelas mousse 70
matelas pneumatique 70
médecin 58
médiator 67
mélangeur 20
melon brodé 26
melon d'eau 27
melon miel 26
menton 4
mer 46
Mercure 44
météorite 45
métronome 66
miel 23
millet 33
minichaîne stéréo 17
minuteur 21
miroir 12
mitaine 9
mitaine isolante 20
mobile 12
moineau 35
monstre 74
montagne 46
montgolfière 53
moteur 52
moto 54
motomarine 51
mouche 31
moufette 35
moule 29
moule à muffins 21
moule à tarte 21
moulin à poivre 23
mouton 32
muguet 42
mulot 35
multiplication 64
mûres 27
muscle 5
mygale 36

N

nacelle 11, 53
nageur 69
nappe 22
navet 24
navette spatiale 45
navire porte-conteneurs 51
nectarine 26
neige 49
Neptune 45
neuf 64
nez 4, 52
niche 31
noix 27
noix de coco 27
nombril 4
nouvelle Lune 44
nuage 49
nuage de cendres 47
nuage en entonnoir 48

O

oasis 47
oie 32
oignon 25
olives 25
ombre à paupières 15
ongle 4
orange 26, 62
orchidée 42
ordinateur 61
oreille 4
oreiller 12
orge 33
orignal 35
orteil 4
os 5, 31
ours 35
ours en peluche 12
oursin 38
ouvre-boîtes 21
ouvrier de voirie 58
ovale 63
œil 4, 48
œillet 42
œuf 28
œufs de Pâques 73

P

pachycephalosaure 40
pagaie 51
pain blanc 28
pain pita 28
palmes 38
palmier 39
pamplemousse 26
panais 24
panier 29, 69
panier à linge 13
pansement adhésif 14
pantalon molletonné 9
pantoufle 13
papaye 27
papier aluminium 28
papier d'emballage 72
papier hygiénique 14
papiers-mouchoirs 14
papillon 31
parallélogramme 63
parasauroloph 41
parasol 39
parc 57
pare-brise 55
parfum 15
passage à niveau 54
passage pour piétons 57
passoire 20
pastilles d'aquarelle 19
patate 24
pâte à modeler 18
patère 13
pâtes alimentaires 28
patin à roues alignées 68
patin de patinage artistique 68
paume de la main 5
paupière 4
pavillon 66
peau 26
pêche 26
pédale 54
pédales 66
peigne 15
pélican 39
pelle 38
pelle mécanique 58
pellicule plastique 28
pelouse 10
pendule 60
pépin 26
père Noël 74
perforatrice 60
perroquet 30
perruche 30
personnage à assembler 18
pèse-personne 14, 58
pétale 42
pétards 72
petites voitures 18
petits pois 25
petits pots 28
pétrolier 50
peuplier 34
phare 51, 55
pharmacie 14
phoque 38
piano 66
pic 35
pichet 22
pied 4
pied de lit 12
pieuvre 39
pigeon 31
pile 71
pilote 58
pin 34
piñata 73
pince 36
pince à cheveux 15
pince-notes 60
pinceau 19
pioche 33
piquet 71
pirate 75
piscine creusée 11
piscine hors sol 11
pissenlit 42
pizza 23
plafonnier 13
plage 46
planche à découper 21
planche à dessiner 18
planche à neige 69
planche à roulettes 68
planche de surf 38
planétarium 44
plante 43
plaque à pâtisserie 21
plateau 46
pleine Lune 44
pleurer 7
pluie 49
pluie forte 49
pluie verglaçante 49
Pluton 45
pneu 55
poche 9, 36
poêle à frire 21, 70
poignet 4
poire 26
poireaux 25
poisson 23
poisson rouge 30
poisson-clown 38
poisson-papillon 38
poivron 25
polo 8
pomme 26
pommes de terre 24
pompier 59
porc 32
porc-épic 35
porte 11, 13, 71
porte-bûches 17
porte-gomme 61
porte-mine 61
poste de police 56
pot 15
pot de crème glacée 28
pot de yogourt 28
poubelle 10
pouce 5
pouf 16
poulailler 32
poule 32
poulet 29
poumons 5
poupe 50
poupée 18
poussette 18
poussin 32
presse-agrumes 21
princesse 74
printemps 48
protège-lame 68
proue 50
pruneau 27
prunes 26
pull molletonné 9
pulpe 27
punaises 60
pupille 4
pupitre à musique 67
pyjama 9
pyramide 63

Q

quartier 27, 44
quatre 64
queue 26, 32, 52
quille 68

R

racine 25, 34, 43
radiocassette laser 13
radis 24
ragoût 23
raie 39
raisin sec 27
raisins 27
rame de métro 55
ramequin 22
ramper 6
ramure 34
râpe 21
rapporteur d'angle 60
raquette de badminton 68
raquette de tennis 68
raquette de tennis de table 68
rasoir électrique 15
rasoir jetable 15
rat 30
râteau 10
rayon de miel 33
réchaud 70
rectangle 63
réfrigérateur 20
règle 61
reliure à anneaux 61
reliure spirale 61
remise 10
renne 74
requin 38
restaurant 56
rétroprojecteur 60
réveil 12
rhamphorynchus 41
rhinocéros 37
rhubarbe 24
rideau 12
rideau de douche 14
rince-bouche 14
rire 7
riz 28
robe 8
robinet 14
robot 74
roi 74
rose 42
rosée 48
rouge 62
rouge à lèvres 15
rouge-gorge 35
rouleau à pâtisserie 21
ruban 73
ruban adhésif 19
ruche 33
rue 57
rutabaga 24

S

sabot 32
sac 58
sac à dos 60
sac à surprises 72
sac cadeau 73
sac de biscuits 28
sac de congélation 28
sac de couchage 70
salade 23
saladier 22
salami 29
salière 23
salopette 8
sandale 8
sandwich 23
sapin 34
satellite 45
Saturne 45
saucière 22
saucisse 29
saumon 29
sauter 6
sauterelle 31
savon 14
saxophone 66
scooter 54
scorpion 36
seau 38
sécateur 43
sèche-cheveux 15
sécheuse 15
selle 54
semelle 8
sept 64
serin 30
serpent à sonnette 36
serpentin 21
serpentins 72
serviette 15, 22
serviette de plage 38
shampooing 14
short 9
siège de sécurité pour enfant 54
siège de vélo pour enfant 54
silo 33
sirop d'érable 23
six 64
skieur alpin 69
skieur de fond 69
slip 9
slip de bain 9
socle 16
soldat 75
Soleil 44
sommet 46
sonde spatiale 45
sorcière 74
soupière 22
sourire 7
souris 61
sous 7
sous-marin 50
soustraction 64
spaghetti 23
sphère 63
spinosaure 41
sprinteuse 69
station spatiale internationale 45
station-service 57
steak 23
stégosaure 40
stéthoscope 58
stylo-bille 61
stylo-plume 61
sucre 23
sucrier 22
sur 7
surligneur 61
synthétiseur 66
système de jeux vidéo 19

T

T-shirt 8
table 16
table à langer 12
table de chevet 13
table de pique-nique 71
tableau 60
tablette de chocolat 29
tablier 20
taille-bordures 10
taille-crayon 61
talon 8
tambourin 67
tamia 35
tapis 12
tarte 23
tasse 22, 70
tasse à mesurer 21
télécommande 17
téléphone 17
télescope 44
télescope spatial Hubble 44
téléviseur 17
tentacule 39
tente 71
tente-caravane 71
Terre 44
tête 4
tête de lit 12
théière 22
thermomètre 49
thorax 4
tige 43
tigre 37
tique 36
tire-bouchon 21
tiroir 20
toile d'araignée 31
toilette 14
toit 11
tomate 25
tondeuse 10
torchon 21
tornade 48
tortillas 28
tortue 30
toundra 46
toupie 18
tour d'habitation 56
tour de contrôle 52
tournesol 42
tournevis 10
tracteur 32, 52
train 55
train miniature 18
traîneau 74
trampoline 69
tramway 55
transbordeur 52
transplantoir 43
trapèze 11, 63
travaux 57
traversier 50
triangle 63, 67
tricératops 41
tricycle 11
trois 64
trombones 60
trompe 37
trompette 66
tronc 34
trotteur 18
trottoir 57
tuba 66
tulipe 42
tunique 25
tunnel 6
tuque 9
tuyau d'arrosage 10
tuyau d'incendie 59
tyrannosaure 41

U

un 64
Uranus 45
usine 57
ustensiles de campeur 70

V

vache 32
vallée 46
vautour 36
veau 33
ventilateur 16
ventouse 39
ventre 4
Vénus 44
verglas 49
vernis à ongles 15
verre 22
verre à vin 22
vert 62
vinaigre de vin 29
violet 62
violon 67
vivarium 30
voie ferrée 54
voile 50
voilier 50
voiture 55
voiture de course 58
voiture de police 59
voiturette 11
volant 68
volcan 47

X

xylophone 67

Y

yacht 51

Z

zèbre 37
zeste 27
zone scolaire 57